Equilibrium and Disequilibrium

Equilibrium and Disequilibrium

A Quantitative Analysis of Economic Interaction

Michael Allingham
Associate Professor of Economics
University of Pennsylvania

Ballinger Publishing Company ● Cambridge, Mass.
A Subsidiary of J.B. Lippincott Company

International Standard Book Number: 0-88410-252-1

Printed in the United States of America

Library of Congress Catalog Card Number: 73-9639

Library of Congress Cataloging in Publication Data

Allingham, Michael.
    Equilibrium and disequilibrium.
    Based in part on the author's thesis, Edinburgh, 1969.
    Includes bibliographical references.
    1. Equilibrium (Economics) 2. Economics—Mathematical models. I. Title.
HB145.A44   338.5'   73-9639
ISBN 0-88410-252-1

Contents

List of Tables

Preface

The combination of deductive and inductive method in economics is typically in that order: first theorize, then observe. Nevertheless, the learning process may be more dialectical, with either component starting the chain; so it was with this book. The quantitative model (Part II) is an immediate simplification of my doctoral dissertation written at Edinburgh (1967-69). The conceptual framework to see this in, and the relevance of the resulting analysis (Parts I and III), were developed subsequently at Essex (1969-71), Northwestern (1971-72), and Pennsylvania (1972-73). I owe much to colleagues at these and other universities for stimulation of the ideas developed in this book—so much that it is impractical to detail. One person however stands out, both intellectually and personally: Michio Morishima. I am deeply grateful to him for introducing me to economic theory as I understand it. I would also like to thank the editors of *Econometrica* for giving me permission to incorporate some work previously published in that journal.

This book is dedicated to Jane.

Philadelphia   April 1973

Part I

Concepts

Chapter One

Introduction

This book presents a quantitative analysis of economic interaction, or general equilibrium econometrics. More specifically, it proposes a fully specified model of an economy in which the formation of equilibrium is completely explained by the independent optimizing behavior of individual agents. This involves a fundamental reformulation of the concepts of station and movement— or equilibrium and disequilibrium.

This introductory chapter first discusses the nature and relevance of the problem, by way of a historical review, and then outlines the approach to be taken, as a plan of the book.

1.1 HISTORICAL REVIEW

Economic science, as all science, is based on both deductive and inductive logic. The review commences with a discussion of the deductive approach, working in the general framework proposed by Walras, then turns to the inductive.

Framework

Although precursors may be traced back as far as one has patience, the founding of economic science in its full, general equilibrium, sense can be unmistakably attributed to Walras, in the 1870s. The lasting value of Walras' contribution lies in the framework he proposed and the questions he asked.

Walras' basic framework is made up of a number of independent agents, each of whom responds to his environment, which is a system of prices, by taking some action which he considers most desirable of those open to him. This is applied to the four areas of exchange, production, accumulation, and money; for the most part we shall consider only the 'canonical' area of production. The agents are now partitioned into producers and consumers. Producers purchase commodities and transform these into other commodities, which they sell;

3

they do this so as to maximize their profit (at the given prices) subject to their given production possibilities. Consumers exchange commodities with each other and with producers to achieve the most desirable (in some given sense) consumption bundle, subject to the value (at the given prices) of their purchases not exceeding that of their sales plus their shares in the producers' profits.

The first question Walras considered was that of the existence of equilibrium: does there exist some set of prices at which all this independent optimizing behavior is in some sense consistent? Walras attempted to answer this affirmatively by demonstrating the equality between the number of (independent) equations and of unknowns in the system. In fact, he was not able to answer this question.

The next question considered was that of stability: given some arbitrary system of prices, is the economy able to move from this to the equilibrium system? Walras perceived the essential point that to ask this question it is necessary to specify some dynamic process; he did this through his famous and imaginative concept of the tatonnement. This has two fundamental aspects: the idea of recontract, which is that all agents' responses to a price system are provisional and will be retracted if the system is not in equilibrium, so there is no trade out of equilibrium, and the introduction of an auctioneer who changes prices according to the state of the provisional market. However, although he attempted to do so, Walras was not able to answer this question satisfactorily for an economy with more than two commodities.

Walras final aim was to answer the questions of comparative statics: how do the equilibrium prices and quantities vary with the underlying parameters of the system, for example, resources, preferences, and production possibilities? Again, little specific progress was made on this question.

Equilibrium

A rigorous examination of the existence problem did not take place until the 1930s, when a number of writers recognized that the problem was much deeper than one of counting equations and unknowns. The problem was solved by Wald, but in a relatively narrow form, and with the use of a rather complex mathematical argument. Happily, the 1940s saw the development in mathematics of various fixed-point theorems, notably that of Kakutani, which were able to generalize and simplify Wald's results. The essence of this approach is to define a mapping from the set of (normalized) prices onto itself, and show that this fulfills the conditions of Kakutani's theorem, so having a fixed point—which is identified with an equilibrium. This was recognized by a number of writers in the 1950s, the most complete statement being the classical work of Debreu.

A completely different approach originated with von Neumann and Morgenstern's work on the theory of games in the 1940s. This treats the agents as players in a cooperative game: there is no concept of prices, and any degree of collusion is allowed. However, the relevant equilibrium concept, that of the core, or the set of all unblocked allocations, was not formalized until the 1950s (though in fact this is implicit in Edgeworth's work of the 1880s). The existence problem then becomes that of showing that the core is not empty, but the more interesting problem is that of identifying the core with the competitive equilibrium: that is showing that the core always contains the equilibrium, and further, shrinks to only this in the limit when the number of agents is increased without bound in some appropriate way. This is shown by various writers in the 1950s and 1960s, the most straightforward demonstration being that of Debreu and Scarf.

The discussion so far has only been concerned with the existence of equilibrium, and has not considered how one might ever compute such an equilibrium, nor whether it will be unique. Algorithms for the first problem were developed in the 1960s, notably by Scarf, while the second was essentially solved in Wald's existence work of the 1930s.

Finally, the equilibrium problem has been posed in a continuous framework in the 1960s and 1970s, most notably by Aumann. This approach considers the set of agents as an atomless measure space, and leads to some powerful and elegant results along the lines of those of Debreu and Scarf. This is the area of most current work.

Stability

Walras' inadequately solved stability problem, for more than two commodities, was first returned to in the 1930s, by Hicks, who developed various sufficient conditions for local stability. In the 1940s Samuelson pointed out that Hicks' concept of stability was not properly dynamic, and developed an alternative (though the two later transpired to be equivalent in some interesting cases). These two contributions stimulated a substantial amount of work on local stability in the 1940s and 1950s. The essence of this approach is to approximate the adjustment process, indicated by the tatonnement mechanism and the demand and supply functions, by a linear map, or matrix, in the neighborhood of equilibrium; stability then depends on the characteristic roots of this matrix, specifically on whether these have negative real parts.

The 1950s also saw the start of work on global stability, by Arrow, Block, and Hurwicz, which again stimulated much subsequent work in the 1950s and 1960s. This approach is based on Lyapounov's stability theorem (which appeared in Russian in the 1890s): it proposes some positive definition function of prices (or some other variable), and attempts to show that this is decreasing over time; stability then follows from the Lyapounov theorem. These extensions of both local and global stability are summarized by Negishi [3].

Finally, stability without tatonnement assumption has been considered in the 1960s and 1970s, this development originating with Negishi [2]. There are two aspects of tatonnement to be replaced: the auctioneer, and recontract; a nontatonnement process therefore requires the specification of who changes prices (and how), and how disequilibrium trade takes place. This is the area of most current work.

Comparative Statics

Comparing equilibria is in some sense the final aim of the analysis, for while the existence and stability questions are logically prior, it is this which generates meaningful theorems. The question was first taken up, in a rigorous general equilibrium framework, by Hicks and by Samuelson in the 1930s and 1940s, where it was closely connected with these authors' work in stability.

The basic method of local comparative statics is to approximate the equilibrium conditions in the neighborhood of equilibrium by a linear equation, and attempt to solve this—or (partially) invert its matrix. Of course to do this one needs some restrictions on the matrix; these may be obtained in four ways. Firstly, there is the maximization hypothesis, that such restrictions might be implied by the second-order conditions of some maximization problem; this has not turned out to be particularly useful as many systems do not fit this form. Secondly, there is the correspondence principle, that restrictions may be implied by the assumption of stability; this has not been as fruitful as expected, because most available stability conditions are sufficient rather than necessary, and therefore too wide. Thirdly, there is qualitative economics, which attempts to infer comparative static (and stability) information from a priori restrictions on the sign pattern of the matrix; however, most results here are rather pessimistic. Finally, there are specific economic restrictions, such as those implied by 'Walras' law' and the homogeneity of demand and supply functions; while these two are valuable, there are not many other apparent restrictions. This whole field is summarized by Allingham and Morishima.

Global results are as relevant in comparative statics as in stability. Work has been done on this in the 1960s and 1970s, originating from that of Morishima [2]. There is however no general method available; each problem is therefore fundamentally different. This is the area of most current work.

Empirical

The work considered so far has been purely theoretical, and not empirically implementable. There are good reasons for this, both practical and conceptual: at a practical level general equilibrium econometrics requires observation of the multitude of individual agents, and at a conceptual level the measurement of tatonnement stability requires observation of (recontracted) actions which never take place.

There is however one empirically implementable approach to general equilibrium, that of input-output analysis, developed in the 1940s in the classic work of Leontief. This provides a deep, and estimatable, insight into the structure of production, at the cost of some drastic simplification, which takes three forms. Firstly, consumers play no real part in the model: final demand is given exogenously. Secondly, there is only one nonproduced resource—usually identified as labor. Finally, production processes are very simple: there are constant returns to scale, no possibility of substitution between inputs, and no joint production. (Some of these restrictions have been relaxed in later work, but the model remains essentially one of physical rather than behavioral relations, or of processes rather than choice.)

Since consumption is autonomous and production takes this simple form, the model may be reduced to a matrix, whose elements are input-output coefficients—giving the input of some commodity required for the output of a unit of some other. These coefficients, and therefore the model they define, may be estimated relatively simply.

If the model can be estimated it may be expected to have an equilibrium (in the appropriate sense, that is be producible); also, theoretical conditions for producibility of abstract models are available. Since demand and supply functions have no meaning, one cannot consider stability in the Walrasian (price) sense; however, it may be considered in an alternative (quantity) sense, though the two are not properly comparable. On the other hand, comparative statics is relatively straightforward: the effect on requirements of some given change in demand is simply obtained by solving the linear system.

Thus while the Leontief model is a major step forward it is still deficient in a number of important ways. This study may be considered as an alternative.

1.2 PLAN OF THE STUDY

The approach to the problem draws from much of the work mentioned above. The book is divided into three parts: concepts, model, and analysis. This section outlines the nature and relevance of these.

Concepts

Part I discusses the general nature of the problem and the concepts it embodies, the present chapter serving as a simple introduction to these.

Chapter 2 looks at some of these concepts more deeply, for it transpires that a fundamental reformulation of the ideas of equilibrium and stability is helpful, if not essential, to the approach to be developed. This is first done in a rather abstract framework, where it is compared with some of the alternative approaches mentioned in the preceding section; later, this is made more specific in a reasonably detailed examination of an exchange economy.

Part I as a whole gives a well-defined, but abstract, concept of an economic model in which the formation of equilibrium is completely explained by the independent optimizing behavior of individual agents.

Model

Part II applies the abstract concept developed in Part I to a concrete economy. This has three aspects: the specification and observation of some real economy to apply the concept to; the more specific interpretation of the model vis-à-vis this economy; and the fitting together of these first two aspects.

Chapter 3 concerns the real observed economy. It commences with a discussion of the general framework in which this is to be observed: specifically, the important specification of who are the agents in the economy, and what variables represent their actions. Once this is decided, these variables, or at least the best approximations available, are obtained for each agent over an interval of time: first for the producing agents, then for the consuming. Finally, some relevant constants, or directly observable parameters, are obtained.

Chapter 4 specifies a theoretical model of the concrete economy, that is an action rule for each of the agents; since this is at a theoretical level it naturally cannot be complete—that is it involves a number of unknown parameters. Before considering individual agents, the general approach is presented, placing the agents' models in context. The individual agents' models are then presented, both for producers and consumers, the chapter concluding with a summary of the model as a whole.

Chapter 5 completes the specification of the concrete model by relating the theoretical model to the observed economy; in other words it estimates, by some appropriate method of statistical inference, the unknown parameters of the theoretical model (and modifies these in the light of experience when necessary). Clearly, the method of inference is important, and this is considered first. It is then applied to the individual agent's models, and the resulting estimates (and necessary modifications) are discussed—again for producers and consumers separately.

Part II as a whole, then, provides a completely specified model of economic interaction, or a tool for quantitative analysis. Related to this, Appendix A lists the specific notation of this part, and Appendix B presents the numerical estimates.

Analysis

Part III uses the tool developed in Part II to obtain some partial and general equilibrium properties by 'solving' the various agents' models individually. The main purpose of this is to test these to see whether they are sufficiently valid to be incorporated in the general equilibrium framework. Chapter 6 commences with a consideration of what is meant by this validity, or the theory of prediction and assessment. However, before this may be applied it is necessary to numerically solve the individual models, a process which is far from automatic; this is discussed next. Finally, the actual predictions are described and interpreted.

Chapter 7 turns to the more interesting general equilibrium properties, by solving all the models simultaneously. This would be impractical if attacked directly, but one is able to use the natural tatonnement process whereby the economy itself solves these equilibrating relations—thereby obtaining results on stability at the same time as on comparative statics. We first discuss this dynamic process in more detail, then consider the measurement of stability and some actual results, and conclude with some full general equilibrium solutions and their relevance.

Chapter 8 draws together the more important points that have materialized. It commences with a discussion of the general implications of the book, then takes up two potential applications in more depth: these relate to decentralized planning, and to collusion and exploitation; the chapter ends with some brief concluding remarks.

Part III as a whole demonstrates the types of results which are available through the method—by solving the models. The solutions themselves are given in Appendix C.

Chapter Two

Economic Models

Before proceeding to the specific building and use of a model of the economy it is important to understand the nature of such models, and of the concepts of equilibrium, stability, and so forth, at a more abstract level. Since this study is one of equilibrium and disequilibrium (or stability) this is of fundamental importance. In this chapter we shall therefore investigate these concepts in depth, and show that they are essentially interrelated. This is important because the interpretation of these concepts differs from the standard interpretation, which defines equilibrium independently from stability.

We commence with the interpretation of a model of an economy, and of equilibrium and stability considered here, and then compare this with the more standard interpretations, concluding with an example, that of the theory of exchange. (A more rigorous treatment, and an extension of the exchange model to include production, is given by Allingham [2].)

2.1 EQUILIBRIUM AND STABILITY

Equilibrium is most naturally defined as a state of balance, that is a state from which there is no movement. Such a concept must therefore depend on the laws of movement, or dynamics, and thus on the concept of stability. It follows that one cannot validly even define equilibrium in an economy without at the same time defining stability. The purpose of this section is to develop this argument, or more specifically to formulate a model of an economy in which the concepts of equilibrium and stability are naturally and interdependently defined, and in which the formation of, or movement towards, equilibrium is completely explained by the independent optimizing behavior of individuals.

Agents

An economy consists of a number of agents, that is consumers, producers, and so on, together with their economic attributes. A model of an economy is an explanation of the actions of the various agents of the economy, that is their demands for commodities, production plans, and so on, and thus of the state of the economy itself. There are many institutional frameworks in which an economy may operate, but for simplicity we shall consider only that at the heart of economic theory: the finite, competitive, selfish, certain economy. This is the economy where there are a finite number of agents who neither cooperate nor are affected by each others' well-being, and who do not recognize uncertainty; it is of course an abstraction from reality, but a useful one to start from.

A description of the economy must start with the specification of the agents, and their characteristics and actions. At this level of abstraction one need only label the agents, say by the index $i = 1, \ldots n$. Similarly, one need not be specific about the characteristics of the agent labelled i, but may represent these by some element x^i of the totality of such characteristics, X; the nature of these is discussed below. An action taken by the agent is represented by an element y^i of his action space Y^i.

So far, the discussion has been purely formal, and has done nothing but attach convenient labels to various entities. Now, however, one comes to economics, in the specification of how the agent chooses his action. This is the heart of economics, and indeed the use of 'chooses' in the preceding sentence almost presupposes the answer: it is that the agent takes the action (or actions) which is the most preferred of all the actions available to him, or 'economizes.'

This immediately requires a concept of preference, which is taken as an axiom: each agent i is able to say of any pair of actions y^i and y'^i in his action space that y^i is at least as preferred as y'^i (which for brevity is written as $y^i \gtrsim^i y'^i$) or that y'^i is at least as preferred as y^i (that is $y^{i'} \gtrsim^i y^i$), or both. From the intuitive idea of preference one also requires that the relation be reflexive (that is $y^i \gtrsim^i y^i$) and transitive (that is that if $y^i \gtrsim^i y'^i$ and $y'^i \gtrsim^i y''^i$ then $y^i \gtrsim^i y''^i$). This preference relation on the action space is one of the characteristics of the agent, and is embodied in x^i.

The remaining characteristics of the agent, usually termed his endowment, determine the other requirements for him to be able to choose in this way, that is determine the actions available to him. Such characteristics are typically such quantities as the amount of wealth the agent has, or the technology open to him. The model would be sterile if the agent's characteristics were the only quantities determining the actions available to him, or his choice set, for then there would be no interaction between agents. It is more natural for the actions of all the other agents to be involved in this, so that, for example, if one agent fixes a high price for his product then other agents will be able to purchase less of this. If the actions of all these other agents are represented by the $(n-1)$-tuple $y^{(i)} \equiv (y^1, \ldots y^{i-1}, y^{i+1}, \ldots y^n)$, then one may formally write the choice set as being given by some correspondence $\varphi^i(x^i, y^{(i)})$.

The agent's action, or actions (as there may be more than one most desirable available action) is then the action(s) in the choice set given by $\varphi^i(x^i, y^{(i)})$ which is most preferred—according to the ordering $\succsim^i$. Formally, this is

$$\left\{ y^i \in Y^i \mid y^i \succsim^i y'^i (\forall y'^i \in \varphi^i(x^i, y^{(i)})) \right\},$$

which rule specifies a correspondence from combinations of the agents' characteristics and other agent's actions, that is $X \times Y^{(i)}$, to the agent's action space, Y^i. Since for the most part the characteristics x^i may be taken as fixed, and a correspondence defined on other agents' actions $Y^{(i)}$ may clearly be represented by one on all agents' actions $Y = Y^i \times Y^{(i)}$, this action rule will be represented by some correspondence $f^i : Y \to Y^i$.

If this is to determine the choice the agent makes then it must consist of something, that is the above set must be nonempty; one must ensure this in specifying the details of the model. If this is to specify the choice uniquely, then the set must be singleton; this would simplify matters (and the later quantitative analysis has this form), but would unduly narrow the scope of the discussion at this general level.

By specifying the agents, their characteristics, and their actions the mechanics of the model are now fully described. It follows that the state of the economy, for example all demands, outputs, and so on, is given by the actions (demands, outputs) of the individual agents, that is by some n-tuple $y \equiv (y^1, \ldots y^n)$; this of course will depend on the characteristics of the whole of the economy, that is on the n-tuple $x \equiv (x^1, \ldots x^n)$.

Equilibrium

One may now consider the basic question of what is an equilibrium state, that is what are the states at which the economy will be at rest, or in balance. Since the economy is nothing but the totality of the agents comprising it, it will be in balance if and only if each agent is in balance, or does not move— that is change his action. This of course requires the specification of how agents, and thus the economy, move, or the dynamic structure of the model.

This is defined perfectly naturally: an agent moves, for example by changing his consumption or production plans, if so doing takes him to a higher level of preference. Since agents do not cooperate, the move must be unilateral, that is take the agent to a higher preference level provided that the environment (and in particular all other agents) does not change. Without any real loss of generality, we assume a certain inertia, that is that an agent does not bother to move to an equally preferred position, only to a strictly preferred one.

It follows that each state generates a further state, or states, in this natural way. Given the present state of the economy, say y, (and some fixed characteristics x^i) agent i will take the action(s) $f^i(y)$. If this is unique then the resulting state of the economy is simply the n-tuple $(f^1(y), \ldots f^n(y))$, denoted $f(y)$; if $f^i(y)$ consists of several equally desirable actions then more generally the state of the economy $f(y)$ is the cartesian product $f^1(y) \times \ldots f^n(y)$. By repeating this process one sees that the state y generates the sequence of sets of states

$$(y, f(y), f(f(y)), \ldots) .$$

It is more convenient to think of this as the set of all sequences of individual states which may be generated by the state y, that is all sequences of states where each element may be generated by its predecessor, or formally,

$$\{(y(0), y(1), y(2), \ldots) \mid y(t) \in f(y(t-1))\} ,$$

where for consistency y is written as $y(0)$. It is clear from the assumption of inertia that if the state y is one of the states which can be generated by y, then it will in fact be generated, that is if $y \in f(y)$ then $f(y) = \{y\}$. Equilibrium may then be more concisely defined as a state which generates itself. (Note that the various $f(y)$ need not be feasible for the economy as a whole, but that because of recontract this does not matter; however, if y, or $f(y)$, is an equilibrium then of course it is feasible for the economy as a whole.)

Stability
This discussion immediately makes clear the fundamental inter-dependence between equilibrium and stability, for the former depends on the generating process, which is essentially the latter—that is to say stability, or instability, is a direct property of the generating, or dynamic, process. A state y^0 is said to be stable with respect to some given y, distinct from y^0, if every sequence of states generated by y has y^0 as its limit; it is stable if this holds for all possible y. Note that throughout no metric is imposed on the set Y, and by using the generalized concept of a net this may still be avoided when talking about limits. However, in most cases Y will be a metric space, so convergence is simpler; if this does apply then one immediately has the concept of local stability, y^0 being locally stable if it is stable with respect to all y sufficiently close to y^0. These are the most common types of stability, sometimes referred to as asymptotic stability; related concepts may be defined analogously.

Tatonnement
It is apparent that the implied dynamic structure of this model embodies a certain myopia of the agents, in that each agent takes his environment as given, and does not attempt to foresee changes in this. For example, if the current environment dictates that a producer should invest heavily in capital goods he will not be deterred by considerations of a different environ-

ment in the next stages of the process. This will be rational if one assumes that no actions are consummated at any state other than an equilibrium, so 'actions' are really 'declarations of intended actions.' This in turn means that there is no need to remember past environments or actions, or equivalently that one may legitimately consider characteristics as fixed during the dynamic process. What one has then is the essence of Walras' concept of tatonnement: a process of declarations or imaginary actions, or of actions in 'imaginary time.'

This is a somewhat abstract, but by no means novel, concept: it is used not only by Walras, but also in Hicks' explanation of adjustment on 'Mondays' with actions for the rest of the 'week,' and Samuelson's continuous version of this. It is nevertheless important to clarify the idea of time used here. Nowhere in the formulation of the dynamic process is reference made to time, but only to sequences of the form

$$(y, f(y), f(f(y)), \ldots),$$

or

$$(y(0), y(1), y(2), \ldots).$$

Such sequences are merely functions from the set of nonnegative integers to the set Y, so one does not need to define any concept of time. One may of course interpret the integers here as measuring some form of time, but if so then this is the *definition* of time—it is no more related to the movement of physical clocks than is any other sequence.

It follows then that if one wants to introduce the 'real' time which is associated with clocks, then the former concept should be called by some different name. Indeed, many models of an economy will include this real time as one of the characteristics of the agents, which is legitimate, since X may be any set. The example of myopia given above then is in no sense one of stupidity: the producer's investment decision may well depend on his beliefs of the future in real time, and may change through real time, but since there is no connection between real time and the imaginary time that one may associate with the dynamic process, the investment decision will not depend on the latter. (It is of some interest to note that a similar way of separating the two forms of time more completely than in, and independently of, Hicks' and Samuelson's formulations was originally proposed by Morishima [1] in Japanese.)

Existence
Now that the concepts of equilibrium and stability have been defined one may consider their properties, at an abstract level. Firstly, it is immediate that a stable state is an equilibrium, for such a state can only generate itself. However, there is some relevance to the two concepts (which

there would not be if they were equivalent), for, as will be seen, an equilibrium need not be stable. More important though is that, for the whole discussion to be nonvacuous, there must exist a state which is an equilibrium. It is simple to show that if no further structure is imposed on the economy an equilibrium need not exist; on the other hand it is also not difficult to provide sufficient conditions for the existence of an equilibrium.

Loosely speaking, one may expect there to be an equilibrium as long as everything is 'smooth,' that is provided that small changes somewhere in the system bring about small changes elsewhere, and provided that combinations of desirable and feasible quantities are also desirable and feasible. More precisely, if the space Y is a nonempty, compact, convex subset of some (finite dimensional) euclidean space and the correspondence $f(y)$ is upper-semicontinuous with (nonempty) convex images $f(y)$, then the conditions of Kakutani's theorem apply to the correspondence $f: Y \rightarrow Y$, so that this has some fixed point, that is there is some y which is an element of its image, or $y \in f(y)$. Because of inertia this means that $f(y) = \{y\}$, so the state y generates itself and is therefore an equilibrium.

Comparative Statics

The model specified can now give comparative statical information. Comparative statics compares the equilibria of two economies whose characteristics differ in some specified way: for example, one might compare the distribution of consumption and prices before and after some change in tastes. Given two characteristics x and x' all relevant comparative static information is obtained in the sets of equilibria corresponding to these, which one may write as

$$F(x) \equiv \{y \mid y \in f(y;x)\}, \; F(x') \equiv \{y \mid y \in f(y;x')\}$$

The correspondence $F: X \rightarrow Y$ assigning equilibrium states to characteristics may be thought of as the reduced form of the model, while $f($ or $f^1, \ldots f^n)$ is the structural form. Again it is important to note that the term 'statics' is merely a convention and does not imply that (real) time may not change— indeed a change in time is one of the more relevant changes in the characteristics which one may consider.

It is well known that the study of comparative statics without the consideration of stability is not fruitful, for the information gained has no predictive content: that is, it does not indicate where the economy would move to if the specified change in characteristics were made, but only where the economy would be at rest. However, since this formulation combines equilibrium with stability it is clear that one has not only simple comparative statical information, but also complete predictive information. If the economy is observed to be in the equilibrium state y when its characteristics are x, then if the characteristics are changed to x' the new equilibrium position of the economy must be the limit of some sequence of states generated by y (when the characteristics are x'), that is some sequence in the set

$$S = \left\{ (y(0), y(1), y(2), \ldots) \mid y(t) \in f(y(t-1); x') \right\}.$$

The prediction of the new equilibrium position(s) the economy will actually move to is then the set

$$\left\{ \lim s \mid s \in S \right\}.$$

This set may of course be empty, but this does not detract from the validity of the formulation of the model, for it gives the information which is appropriate: that is that the economy does not settle anywhere.

2.2 ALTERNATIVE FORMULATIONS

It is instructive to compare the concepts of equilibrium and stability developed in the preceding section with the standard concepts reviewed in Chapter I: those of the classical (Walras-Debreu) and game theoretic approaches.

Classical

As has been noted, Walras appreciated the fundamental point that a satisfactory model of an economy must not only show what would be an equilibrium, but also how this is to be achieved. However, although Walras recognizes the equivalent logical status of the equilibrium and stability problems, he defines equilibrium independently from stability and then considers how the equilibrium might be reached. This means that equilibrium cannot be defined in the natural way. Instead, it must be defined in a more arbitrary way, which is in terms of certain 'excesses,' that is components (where these exist) of the sums of individual actions, $\sum_{i=1}^{n} y^i$ (in the case where such sums are defined, that is where Y is a linear space). This direct definition of equilibrium in terms of excesses must be arbitrary (relative to the natural or balance sense); it is a property which would typically appear desirable in an equilibrium not of the equilibrium itself. Now it happens that in many cases an equilibrium defined in the natural sense fulfills the condition on the excesses, but this is a fortunate property of these cases, rather than a necessary property of the concept of equilibrium.

This difference may be made clear by a simple example, that of demand and supply in a single competitive market. In such a model the classical *definition* of equilibrium would be that excess demand be zero, or that supply equal demand. If asked to justify this the typical reply might be that if supply exceeded demand then prices would fall, and conversely, which situation would somehow not be characteristic of an equilibrium. In other words, the excess definition would be justified by the natural definition. Under certain plausible assumptions concerning dynamic behavior the two are clearly equivalent, so either approach is satisfactory, but *only if* these dynamic assumptions are specified; for strictly speaking, it is a theorem that the natural condition *plus* the dynamic structure imply the excess condition. Since under other not implausible dynamic assumptions the two are not equivalent, it is important to distinguish between them.

An important application of this relates to the study of unemployment, and indeed most Keynesian economics. Perhaps one reason why this has been such an open area is that the idea of unemployment at equilibrium is without meaning if equilibrium is considered in the excess sense. In the natural sense, however, it is quite consistent, for there is no prior presumption of either full employment or unemployment at equilibrium. To determine which will apply one must consider further the dynamic structure of the model, through the disequilibrium behavior of the various agents. This provides a specific focus for the study of unemployment, removing the conceptual problems and leaving only the (very real) particular problems. (This example is of some relevance here as the specific model developed in Part II will allow for unemployment at equilibrium.)

A further basic difference is that in order to explain the formation of some of the aspects of an equilibrium, and thus to define stability, Walras introduces a new agent, called the 'auctioneer,' whose status is fundamentally different from that of the original agents. Since this new agent is (possibly) imaginary, and in any case is given no explicit optimizing structure, this leads to some obvious difficulties of interpretation; in any event the model no longer explains the formation of equilibrium in terms of the agents' optimizing behavior.

This difference then is essentially related to stability, while the former is related to equilibrium; since equilibrium and stability are interdependent, so are these differences. Although Walras did not formulate the model in this way, one may give the auctioneer an optimizing structure, based on expectations, and thus an action rule, which provides the necessary link, in the form of a dynamic structure, for an equilibrium in the excess sense to be one in the balance sense— at least for some interesting models. (The excess definition of course is meaningless if Y is not a linear space, as may well be the case—for example in models of location, where 'Philadelphia plus Cambridge' is not defined.)

Debreu's formalization of an economy is essentially a more general and rigorous version of Walras', with the basic difference that a dynamic structure is not considered at all. It therefore has the same general characteristics as Walras' model without the auctioneer, which means that it embodies the arbitrary excess definition of equilibrium.

Because it has no dynamic structure it cannot explain the formation of equilibrium states, and therefore does not define a predictive model. Since the components of a state y which would have been determined by the auctioneer in Walras' model are not now determined by any agent, these can never change; there will then typically be many states which are equilibria in the natural sense, but which will not be equilibria in the excess sense. (This fact, that a natural equilibrium may be an excess equilibrium in the Walras model, but not in the same model without its dynamic structure, is one obvious example of the interdependency of the concepts of equilibrium and stability.)

Game Theoretic

It is also instructive to compare these concepts with the game-theoretic alternative to the classical approach. This treats the various agents in the economy as players in a cooperative game, equilibrium being defined in terms of the core of this game, that is the set of allocations which cannot be blocked by any coalition of the players.

It is in this concept of equilibrium that the basic difference to the classical formulation lies, for the core is a natural balance concept—roughly speaking it consists of the states from which no agent wishes to move, in coalition with others if appropriate. It is then a direct cooperative equivalent of the natural equilibrium concept. However, the game approach is also fundamentally different from this approach, for although its equilibrium concept depends on balance it has no dynamic structure; again then it does not explain the formation of an equilibrium, or define a predictive model.

It is important to note that the game theoretic model, although cooperative in the game sense, is still a model of a competitive economy. For example, one of the most interesting results of this approach, when applied to models of exchange, is the identification of an equilibrium in the classical model, which involves prices and no cooperation, with an equilibrium in the game model, which involves cooperation and no prices; and also the reverse identification (in a limiting sense).

Although the natural approach has this basic difference to the game theoretic, one may still specify the model in the mechanism of this, that is as a non-cooperative n-person general sum game in normal form. This involves the specification of a set of players, for each player a strategy set, and a rule (kernel) assigning a numerical value for each player to any n-tuple of players' strategies. The identification is obvious: the set of players is simply the set of agents, and the strategy set of a player is simply his action space, Y^i.

The specification of the kernel, which is a function $v : Y^i \times \ldots Y^n \to R$, requires the assumption that each player's preference relation $\gtrsim^i$ may be represented by some utility function u^i. (A utility function, loosely speaking, assigns increasing numbers to more preferred actions; more formally, it satisfies

$$u^i(y^i) \geqslant u^i(y'^i) \Leftrightarrow y^i \gtrsim^i y'^i \ ,$$

with equality in, and only in, the case of indifference, that is where additionally $y'^i \gtrsim {}^i y^i$.) The value to player i of the strategies $(y^i, \ldots y^n) = y$ is then the highest utility level he may obtain on his choice set—which, being determined by other players' strategies $y^{(i)}$, is $\varphi^i(x^i, y^{(i)})$; formally

$$v^i(y) = \sup\left\{u^i(y^i) \mid y^i \in \varphi^i(x^i, y^{(i)})\right\}.$$

Now the strategies y will constitute an equilibrium if the utility level which each player achieves under this is no less than that which he would obtain under any (possible) unilateral move, that is if, for all i,

$$v^i(y^i, y^{(i)}) \geqslant v^i(y'^i, y^{(i)}) \ (\forall y'^i \in \varphi^i(x^i, y^{(i)})).$$

Expressed in this form it is immediate that the natural concept of an equilibrium is simply that of a Nash equilibrium in a game.

Formally then, there is a close resemblance between the natural and game theoretic approaches, but the interpretation is very different. The main difference is that, because of the myopia or tatonnement nature of the model, agents consider other agents' actions or strategies as given, and so do not act as if they are in conflict, which is the fundamental characteristic of a game. It follows from this that no agent would want to use mixed, or randomized, strategies, so such a concept is redundant: an equilibrium must therefore be a Nash equilibrium in pure strategies, and conversely.

Although the interpretation of the model is very different from that of a game, the formal similarity is useful. For one thing, it simplifies the question of existence of an equilibrium, for this is merely that of the existence of a Nash equilibrium in pure strategies in the game: this makes it clear that many abstract models would not have an equilibrium. A further potential use of this formal similarity is the generalization of the concept of a model to allow, for example, cooperation between agents or an infinite number of agents, for there is a well-developed theory of cooperative and of infinite games.

Example

Finally, consider a simple example of a model expressed in the form of a game. This example has two agents, labelled 1 and 2, each of whose action spaces consist of only two elements, say

$$Y^1 = \left\{y_1^1, y_2^1\right\}, \quad Y^2 = \left\{y_1^2, y_2^2\right\}$$

The kernel v is simply defined by

$$v^1(y_j^1, y_k^2) = v^2(y_j^1, y_k^2) = a_{jk} \quad (j,k = 1,2),$$

where the a_{jk} are the elements of the matrix

It is clear that the pair (y_1^1, y_2^2) is an equilibrium, for

$$v^1 (y_1^1, y_2^2) = 3 > 1 = v^1 (y_2^1, y_2^2)$$

and

$$v^2 (y_1^1, y_2^2) = 3 > 1 = v^2 (y_1^1, y_1^2) \ ,$$

so one has an equilibrium. However, this is not unique, for one may similarly see that (y_2^1, y_1^2) is also an equilibrium. (Note that this second equilibrium is certainly not optimal in any sense, for *both* players are strictly better off under the first.) Which, if either, of these equilibria is stable? Obviously both generate only themselves (as they are equilibria); the pair (y_1^1, y_1^2) may be seen to generate (y_2^1, y_2^2), which in turn generates the original pair, so one has the limitless sequence

$$((y_1^1, y_1^2), (y_2^1, y_2^2), (y_1^1, y_1^2), \ldots) \ ,$$

while the pair (y_2^1, y_2^2) of course generates a similar sequence. Thus no points distinct from either equilibrium generate a sequence with a limit, and so both equilibria are unstable.

From this example and the preceding more general discussion one has the following properties of the abstract model: it may or may not have an equilibrium, and if it does this need neither be unique nor stable, but if there is some stable state this will be an equilibrium. Since the economy is specified only at a very abstract level it is quite natural that one has only these general results; for more concrete results further specifications of the nature of the economy must be made. The purpose of this study is to do this in a quantitative manner.

2.3 THEORY OF EXCHANGE

Before proceeding to an actual observable economy it is instructive to apply the concepts of this chapter to a more specific, yet still theoretical, economy. The example considered is the standard one of the theory of exchange, though the interpretation of this will of course be different. Specifically, we consider a finite, competitive, selfish and certain economy, abstracting from the problems of production, money, and capital. We first describe the nature of this economy and the classical model applied to this, then develop the model in this framework.

Economy

An exchange economy has a number of agents, indexed by $i \in I \equiv \{1, \ldots n\}$, who exchange a number of perfectly divisible commodities, indexed by $h \in H \equiv \{1, \ldots l\}$, these being distinguished by their physical nature, and by their ownership. This is a simple extension of the more standard model which does not distinguish between commodities on the basis of ownership, and so involves no loss of generality; it may indeed be necessary if agents, and thus their commodities, have locations, and location is considered a characteristic of a commodity. It follows that no commodity may be held initially by more than one agent, so one may associate a positive number $l(i)$ of commodities with the agent i, these being the commodities indexed by $h \in H(i)$, where $\{H(i) \mid i \in I\}$ is a partition on H.

Each agent is endowed with positive amounts of the commodities associated with him, that is with a vector of endowments $z^i \equiv \left[z_h \right], h \in H(i)$. The agent exchanges some or all of his endowment for nonnegative amounts of other agents' commodities, that is for a vector or purchases $q^{\underline{i}} \equiv \left[q^i_h \right]$, $h \notin H(i)$, after which he is left with nonnegative amounts of his own commodities, that is with a vector of retentions $q^{\overline{i}} \equiv [q^i_h]$, $h \in H(i)$. He thus obtains the consumption vector $q^i \equiv (q^{\underline{i}}, q^{\overline{i}})$, an element of R^l_+. To choose an optimal consumption the agent has a preference ordering $\succsim^i$ on R^l_+; this is assumed to be continuous, convex, and insatiable in all commodities, so it may be represented by a continuous concave utility function $u^i: R^l_+ \to R$. The characteristics of an agent are then fully described by his endowment and preference ordering, that is by $x^i = (z^i, \succsim^i)$.

Exchange does not take place directly, but rather commodities are bought and sold for amounts of 'credit,' the only restriction being that each agent must have a nonnegative amount of credit after the exchange process. The nonnegative amount of credit for which a unit of a commodity is bought or sold is its price, p_h; the prices of the commodities associated with the agent i are denoted by the vector $p^i \equiv [p_h], h \in H(i)$, and of those not associated with him by $p^{\underline{i}} \equiv [p_h], h \notin H(i)$. A state of the economy is then fully described by the (complete) price vector, $p = (p_1, \ldots p_l)$, together with the consumptions of all the agents, $q = (q^1, \ldots q^n)$, that is by $y = (p, q)$.

Now that one has specified the nature of the characteristics, x, and states, y, of the economy one need only add the agent's decision rule $f^i: Y \to Y^i$, or equivalently his choice set correspondence $\varphi^i: Y \to Y^i$ —since f^i is completely determined by φ^i and his preferences, which are given.

Classical

In the classical model without an auctioneer the agent's action y^i consists of the choice of a consumption vector q^i. The price vector thus forms part of his environment, so, as he must have a nonnegative amount of credit after the exchange process, his choice set, given p, is determined by

$$\varphi^i(\bar{p}) = \left\{q^i \in R_+^l \mid \bar{p}\ q^i \leqslant \bar{p}^i\ z^i\right\}.$$

This completes the specification of the model, though one must additionally define equilibrium: a state (p, q) is an equilibrium if it is characterized by having no positive excess aggregate demands, and negative excess aggregate demands only for free commodities. If aggregate demands are written as $d_h = \sum_{i \in I} q_h^i$, one may express this condition as, for each $h \in H$,

$$p_h > 0 \Rightarrow d_h = z_h,\ p_h = 0 \Rightarrow d_h \leqslant z_h.$$

It is well known that such an equilibrium exists.

Since no agent chooses any price this model provides no explanation of the formation of equilibrium prices. This implies that there is no dynamic process, and therefore no means for investigating stability. It also implies that any state (p, q) can only generate the state(s) (p, q'), which must then generate itself, so for any price vector there is a state from which no agent will prefer to move, and thus an equilibrium in the sense of balance.

The (Walras) classical model with an auctioneer is the same as the preceding model except that a new agent indexed 0 is introduced, whose action consists of the choice of prices, and whose decision rule is

$$f^0(\bar{p}, \bar{d}) = p$$

where

$$p_h/\overline{pb} = \max\left\{\bar{p}_h/\overline{pb} + a_h \bar{d}_h,\ 0\right\}.$$

Here $b \in R_+^l$ is some fixed weight vector, so $\overline{pb} \equiv \bar{P}$ is an overall price index; the a_h are positive constants, so without loss of generality one may choose physical units so as these are all unity. One then has

$$p = \max\left\{\bar{p} + \bar{P}\bar{d},\ 0\right\}$$

(where the maxima are taken component-wise). The auctioneer may be seen as attempting to choose prices which make aggregate excess demands $(d - z)$ zero. His preferences may then be (arbitrarily) defined by

$$p \gtrsim^0 p' \Leftrightarrow \| \hat{d}(p) - z \| \leqslant \| \hat{d}(p') - z \|,$$

where $\hat{d}(p)$ is the market excess demand vector he believes will occur at prices p, and $| \cdot |$ is some norm, on R^l; his choice set is simply R^l_+. For him to be acting rationally he must believe that, having been given a pair $(\bar{p}, \bar{d})$, market demands are given by

$$\hat{d}(p) = \max \left\{ \bar{d} + (\bar{p} - p)/\bar{P}, 0 \right\}.$$

The addition of the auctioneer provides an explanation of the formation of prices, and thus of the equilibrium, so that there is a dynamic process in which stability may be investigated. Further, an equilibrium in the natural sense is now an equilibrium in the excess sense, and vice versa: an equilibrium in the natural sense requires that the auctioneer does not prefer to move, which occurs if and only if all market excess demands are zero (or negative only with zero price); if the auctioneer does not move then no agent's environment changes, so no agent moves. However, the formation of equilibrium in this model depends on the (possibly imaginary) auctioneer; it would be preferable to explain this purely in terms of the agents' behavior.

Natural

To specify the natural model applied to an exchange economy one must specify the choice set correspondences φ^l. We first discuss the general assumptions underlying these: since the formalization differs from that of the classical model it is clear that the general assumptions must do likewise. We restrict the discussion to the differences. The natural model of exchange is based on the axiom that sellers quote prices and buyers take these as given; this may be justified on three grounds. Now if price is to be determined it must be determined by some agent, that is either by buyers or sellers. Firstly then, sellers naturally know the market for their commodities, since they are endowed with the supply and are faced with the demands; buyers on the other hand know only a fraction, that relating to their purchases, of this information. Secondly, prices are the informational channels of the system, and if sellers quote prices only l such channels are required, whereas if buyers quote then nl are required, which is much more cumbersome. Thirdly, that there are n potential buyers but only one seller for each commodity, so (in a loose sense) market power will typically rest with the seller. Note that since all transactions are for credit, rather than barter, the seller in a transaction is well defined; also a buyer cannot resell to compete with a seller, since the commodity would then be changed—for commodities are identified by ownership.

Since a seller has no preferences over prices, he cannot quote so as to directly influence his utility, but only indirectly. The link is through the credit that the ensuing sales will bring him, so for the agent to be able to quote a price rationally he must have an expectation of the amount of this credit, or of the market demand function for his commodities. The natural assumption is that these are the expectations implicit in the behavior of the Walrasian auctioneer. The only knowledge of the environment that this requires is of those parts which directly impinge on the agent: prices, $\bar{p}$, and the market demands expressed to him, $\bar{d}^i \equiv [d_h]$, $h \in H(i)$.

An explanation of these expectations is that the agent is not only endowed with his physical commodities, but also with some inherent notion of their worth, or 'use value'; more specifically, that the agent has some exogenously given belief in the slopes of the demand functions for his commodities.

One may now formalize this in the specification of the choice set correspondence. Since the agent now chooses a price for his commodities and a consumption, an action y^i is a pair (p^i, q^i), and the action space the totality of such pairs, that is $R_+^{1+l(i)}$ (note that preferences are now effectively defined only on a subspace, that of consumptions, of the action space). The choice set itself must now depend on the agent's expectations: by analogy with the auctioneer, the agent, given some environment $(\bar{p}, \bar{d}^i)$, considers market demands, or equivalently his planned sales, to be given by

$$\hat{d}^i(p_h) = \max\left\{\bar{d}^i + (\bar{p}^i - p^i)/\bar{P}, 0\right\}.$$

His choice set is then the set of all prices and consumptions in Y^i which will not leave him a net debtor after exchange. Since this condition is satisfied if the value of his purchases (of other agents' commodities) does not exceed the value of his sales (of his commodities), and since his (planned) retentions are simply his endowments less his (planned) sales, this may be written as

$$\varphi^i(\bar{p}, \bar{d}^i) = \left\{(p^i, q^i) \in R_+^{l+l(i)} \mid q^{\bar{i}} = a^i - d^i, \bar{p}^{\underline{i}} q^{\underline{i}} \leqslant \bar{p}^i \hat{d}^i\right\}$$

where $\hat{d}^i$ is given above (note that the restriction that consumptions are non-negative automatically implies that planned sales cannot exceed endowments).

One must check that the maximization of $\succsim^i$ on φ^i determines a well-defined action rule f^i, or that a maximum exists. Since $\succsim^i$ is continuous by assumption, this will be ensured if the choice set $\varphi^i(y)$ is nonempty, closed, and bounded. Nonemptiness and closedness are obvious, but boundedness less so: this is shown in four parts. Firstly, the implied nonnegativity of $\hat{d}^i$ clearly implies that q^i is bounded. Secondly, if $p_h \geqslant \bar{P}\bar{d}_h + \bar{p}_h$ then $\hat{d}_h$ is zero, that is there is no (planned) trade and so price has no meaning; one may then without loss of generality define the price when there is no trade to be the minimum price ensuring this, that is $\bar{P}\bar{d}_h + \bar{p}_h$, so that p^i is bounded. Thirdly, the nonnegativity of q^i implies the boundedness of $\hat{d}^i$, and thus of $p^i \hat{d}^i$ and $\bar{p}^i q^i$, and so of $q^{\underline{i}}$, provided that $\bar{p}$ is positive. Finally, note that $\bar{p}$ is indeed positive, because if it is generated by the environment $(\bar{p}, \bar{d})$, then $\bar{p}_h \geqslant \frac{1}{2}(\bar{P}\bar{d}_h + \bar{p}_h)$, for otherwise an increase in both q^i and $q^{\bar{i}}$, and thus of utility, could be achieved by an increase in $\bar{p}_h$; since $\bar{\bar{p}}_h$ or $\bar{d}_h$ must be positive, as is $\bar{P}$, this ensures that $\bar{p}_h$ is positive.

The action rule f^i then is well-defined, and since equilibrium is already defined naturally, the model now constitutes a complete model of exchange—that is a complete explanation of the formation of an equilibrium or of the process by which this may be achieved.

Existence

The basic question of the existence of equilibrium, or equivalently of a fixed point of the mapping f, now arises. As was shown in Section 2.1, a sufficient condition for the mapping $\hat{f}: A \rightarrow A$ to have a fixed point is that A be a nonempty, compact, convex subset of some euclidean space, and that $\hat{f}$ be upper semicontinuous and convex valued.

It is clear however that these conditions do not apply to f, since Y is certainly not bounded. One must then find a restricted mapping $\hat{f}: A \rightarrow A$ which does satisfy these conditions, and whose fixed point implies a fixed point for f.

As a start to this, consider the choice set correspondence φ^i. It has been shown that, for any y, its value $\varphi^i(y)$ is nonempty and compact. To show that this is convex one need only show that its projection in q^i, that is $S^i \equiv \{ q^i \mid (p^i, q^i) \in \varphi^i(y) \}$, is convex; this is because p^i is a linear function of q^i, specifically

$$ p^{\bar{i}} / \bar{P} = q^i + \bar{d}^i - z^i + \bar{p}^{\bar{i}} / \bar{P} \ . $$

Using this relation, S^i may be rewritten as

$$ \left\{ q^i \mid \pi^i q^i + q^i q^i \leqslant \lambda^i \right\} $$

where $\pi^i \in R_+^e$ and $\lambda^i \in R_+$ are simply continuous functions of $\bar{p}$ and $\bar{d}^i$; it is immediate that this set is convex. Now since $p^{\bar{i}}$ is a continuous (linear) function of q^i and (π^i, λ^i) is a continuous function of $(\bar{p}, \bar{d}^i)$, the correspondence φ^i taking $(\bar{p}, \bar{d}^i)$ to $\varphi^i(y)$ will be shown to be continuous if the correspondence taking (π^i, λ^i) to S^i is continuous. But continuity of this may be shown in exactly the same way as it is by Debreu for the parallel classical correspondence taking (a, b) to $\{c \mid ac \leqslant b\}$.

It is now clear that individual demands q^i are obtained from the maximization of a continuous function u^i on the compact images $\varphi^i(y)$ of a continuous correspondence φ^i. It follows that the individual demand correspondences, and thus the aggregate, $d(p)$, are upper-semicontinuous. Also, insatiability of preferences implies that demand becomes infinite at zero price. Together, these results imply that demand plus price is bounded away from zero. But one also knows, from the discussion of the boundedness of $\varphi^i(y)$, that $p \geqslant \frac{1}{2} (\bar{P} \bar{d} + \bar{p})$; this means that price is absolutely bounded away from zero (that is it has a positive lower bound which is independent of the environment $(\bar{p}, \bar{q})$).

It would also be desirable to bound prices absolutely from above. This is achieved artificially, by considering the normalized system $\hat{f}: \hat{Y} \to \hat{Y}$, where $\hat{Y}$ is the subset of Y in which all prices sum to unity, and $\hat{f}$ is defined by

$$\hat{f}(\bar{p}, \bar{q}) = \left\{ (p / \underset{h \in H}{\Sigma} p_h, q) \mid (p, q) \in f(\bar{p}, \bar{q}) \right\} .$$

(Note that this does map into $\hat{Y}$.) Now it is clear from the form of the choice set correspondence and the independence of preferences on prices that any positive multiple of an equilibrium price will also be an equilibrium price, specifically.

$$(p, q) \in f(p, q) \Rightarrow (p / \underset{h \in H}{\Sigma} p_h, q) \in f(p / \underset{h \in H}{\Sigma} p_h, q) .$$

It is also clear that if demands do not change then neither need prices, so

$$(p', q) \in f(p, q) \Rightarrow (p, q) \in f(p, q) .$$

It follows that if $\hat{f}$ has an equilibrium then so does f.

Prices are immediately bounded absolutely in $\hat{Y}$, both from above (by unity) and away from zero. The first means that all consumers' incomes, and expenditures, are absolutely bounded, which together with the second implies that all individually feasible demands are absolutely bounded. Instead of considering $\hat{f}: \hat{Y} \to \hat{Y}$ one may then consider its restriction $\hat{f}: A \to A$, where A is some compact, convex subset of $\hat{Y}$ which contains every normalized choice set, that is every $\hat{\varphi}(y) \equiv \varphi(y) \cap \hat{Y}$.

One may now demonstrate equilibrium. Firstly, A is defined to be nonempty, compact, and convex. Secondly, the choice set correspondence φ is continuous with nonempty, compact, convex images, so it is trivial that the normalized choice set correspondence $\hat{\varphi}(y)$ has these same properties. It follows from this that $\hat{f}$ (obtained from the maximization of a continuous function on the compact convex images of a continuous correspondence) is upper-semicontinuous with convex images. Since this is all in a euclidean space, one has fulfilled the conditions ensuring a fixed point for $\hat{f}: A \to A$, and thus for $\hat{f}: \hat{Y} \to \hat{Y}$, and again for $f: Y \to Y$. It follows that there exists an equilibrium.

It may be noted that in an equilibrium one has $p = \bar{p}$, which implies $\hat{d} = \bar{d}$, and $q = \bar{q}$, which implies $d = \bar{d}$; together these implications give $d = \hat{d}$, which means that $d^i + q^i = z^i$ for every agent i. It is thus shown that the classical condition of no excess demands is in fact satisfied in equilibrium.

The question of uniqueness of equilibrium in this model is similar to that in the classical model: to ensure uniqueness one must impose further restrictions, for example strict convexity of preferences, and market demand functions which are decreasing in own prices for all other prices. However, since each agent's choice set is strictly convex in his commodities, and therefore in their prices, any given state of the economy will generate a unique price system, just as does the Walrasian auctioneer.

Stability

The discussion is primarily concerned with the formulation of a model embodying a natural dynamic process and showing that this has an equilibrium, rather than deriving specific conditions for the stability of equilibrium under this process. However, as an illustration, we can demonstrate an interesting comparison between the Walrasian and natural models under some simplifying assumptions.

This concerns local stability in the standard 'canonical' case, that is where preferences are strictly convex so that the action rules f^i are (continuous) functions, which are also assumed to be continuously differentiable.

In general, an agent does not choose prices to maximize his income and then choose an optimal consumption for this income, since he may quote a high price for a commodity partly to consume more of that commodity. However, if the agent's original commodities form only a small part of his consumption, he may find it convenient to separate his functions as seller and as buyer: as a seller he will choose prices to maximize his income, then as a buyer he will purchase an optimal bundle (including possible purchases from himself); it will now be assumed that the agent's behavior may be approximated by such a two-stage process. It is also assumed that, over small changes in time, the agent ignores changes in the overall price index when computing the best price to charge for his commodities. (It is interesting to note that under this assumption the process is close in spirit to that developed by Fisher [2] for 'quasicompetitive' adjustment and formally similar to that of Negishi [1] for monopolistic competition—which is essentially what the model involves.)

To maximize his income, that is $p^{\bar{i}}\, \hat{d}^{\bar{i}}$, subject to not selling more than he has, that is subject to $\hat{d}^i \leqslant z^i$, the agent chooses

$$p^i = \max \ \left\{ \ \tfrac{1}{2}(\bar{P}\,\bar{d}^i + \bar{p}^i), \bar{p}^i + \bar{P}(\bar{d}^i - z^i) \right\}$$

(as may be seen by direct constrained maximization). Rearranging this, one obtains the explicit dynamic process, expressed in a continuous form, as

$$\dot{p}^i = \max \ \left\{ \ \tfrac{1}{2}(Pd^i - p^i), P(d^i - z^i) \right\} \ ,$$

where a dot indicates differentiation with respect to the imaginary time of the process.

For simplicity, consider the case where $\dot{p}_h$ takes its first form, $\dot{p}_h = \tfrac{1}{2}\ P(d_h - p_h)$, for all commodities; this is the interesting form, for it is clear that in the other (boundary) form, $\dot{p}_h = P(d_h - z_h)$, there is no substantive difference between this model and the Walrasian.

Consider then the system $2\dot{p} = Pd - p$, where P is taken as fixed. Taking a linear approximation of this in the neighborhood of the equilibrium p^0 one has

$$\dot{p} = (PD - I)(p - p^0)$$

where $D = [\partial d_i / \partial p_j]$ ($i, j \in H$) is the jacobian of the demand system. The stability of this system is therefore determined by the matrix $PD - I$, in contrast with that of the corresponding Walrasian system $\dot{p} = Dp$, which is of course determined by the matrix D. But it is immediate that the real parts of the characteristic roots of the first matrix are all smaller (by an amount $1/P$) than those of the second. Since stability is equivalent to these real parts all being negative, it follows that the stability of D implies that of $PD - I$, but not conversely. Thus it is shown that (in this simple case) the natural system is strictly more stable than the Walrasian.

Part II

Model

Chapter Three

Observed Economy

The concept of an economic model developed in Chapter 2 must now be applied to a concrete economy. More specifically, one must choose an economy to study, identify the various agents in this economy, and specify an action rule for each of these. Naturally, it will not be possible to specify these completely on theoretical considerations alone: theory will determine the form of these, but leave a number of unknown parameters. These parameters are to be estimated by the appropriate methods of statistical inference from observed reality. This chapter will be concerned with the specification and observation of this reality—the data; Chapter 4 will propose the theoretical model, in terms of various unknown parameters, and Chapter 5 will consider the appropriate methods of inference, and discuss the resulting parameter estimates. Together then, these three chapters will completely specify the mapping f.

It may seem inappropriate to consider the observed economy before the theoretical model, and in a world of perfect information this might be the case. However, in practice the theoretical model must be artificially constrained to include only entities which are actually, not only conceptually, observable. (For example there is no point in attempting to use an agent's accumulated wealth to explain some attribute of his behavior if this wealth is not practically observable and measurable.) To phrase this another way, variables which are observed, even if measured with perfect accuracy, might not exactly coincide with the variables which would ideally be used in the theoretical model. (For example, the latter might find it appropriate to explain an agent's consumption of some commodity, where the actual variable 'consumption' would in fact be his purchases.) Clearly such limitations should be taken account of in specifying the theoretical model—which is why this is done after considering the data. (It should be mentioned at the outset that the notation used in Part II is self-contained, and independent of that of Part I.)

In practice, observable data can only be an approximation to the concepts one is interested in. If such data is used it is then vital that it be fully discussed. This is the purpose of this chapter: it first presents a general framework in which one may relate the data, then proceeds to discuss the details of the variables associated with the models for the various agents—both 'producers' and 'consumers'; it concludes with a discussion of various constants which may more conveniently be considered as 'data.'

3.1 GENERAL CONCEPTS

One must first consider what to observe—that is which economy, which agents in this economy, and what attributes of these agents. The discussion then commences with a specification of the economy, together with an identification of the agents and their action spaces, and concludes with some conventions and notation.

Economy

The concrete economy to which the analysis is applied is taken to be a developed capitalist economy, small enough (geographically) to be reasonably homogeneous. The choice is the economy of the United Kingdom (UK), over the period 1956 through 1966. The geographical choice is arbitrary, but the temporal choice depends more on some practical aspects. General equilibrium analysis requires finely disaggregated data, which is often difficult to obtain, particularly as history recedes. The first year of the observations is the earliest year for which the disaggregated data used was available. The drawback to considering an economy small enough to be reasonably regionally homogeneous is that it will typically be dependent on relations with the rest of the world. The latest year of the observations is the last year in which the prime link with the outside world, the exchange rate (of sterling on dollars), had not changed. This gives an acceptable observation period of eleven years.

Since the relevant concept of equilibrium is that of temporary equilibrium, the economy should be observed as frequently as practical during the observation period. This turns out to be quarterly: figures for shorter periods (months) though ideally preferable, are not available for many variables—as it is, compilation of consistent disaggregated quarterly figures poses many problems.

Agents

It is obvious that in practice only a small number of agents can be considered. In the standard macroeconomic framework three (or four) classes of agent are distinguished: consumers (possibly including the rest of the world), producers, and government.

The most internally distinguishable class of agent is that of producers, where at least ten categories may be identified. These then constitute the ten basic agents. Distinguishing among other agents turns out to be either impossible (because of lack of data) or unnecessary (because the actions themselves—such as consumption, exports, government expenditure—immediately determine the actors). Thus all nonproducing agents, are considered as a single agent—the final demand (or final) agent.

Although many actions are naturally associated with particular agents, this association is in some cases more arbitrary. Bearing this in mind, the action space of a producer is taken to be all those attributes of production which he primarily determines. An explanation of what constitutes these must await the exposition of the theoretical model in Chapter 4. Here these are simply listed: as his output, materials, capital, investment, stocks, labor, unemployment, earnings (of labor), output price, materials price, and profits.

The consumer agent proper is associated with the determination of various categories of consumption and the corresponding categories of consumer prices. The foreign aspect of the consumer is associated with the determination of various categories of exports, imports, and world trade, and the government aspect with four categories of government expenditure, two categories of direct tax rates, and various categories of consumption tax rate.

(It should be stressed that this association of actions with agents is in part purely for convenience, and infers nothing about the plausibility of the theoretical model. While the enumeration of actions is necessary here, the explanation of these is more properly dealt with in Chapter 4.)

The specification of the ten producing agents, or industries, is based on the Standard Industrial Classification (SIC) for 1958, as defined by the Central Statistical Office (CSO) [2]. This is because most published data is based on this, with the SIC order as the finest unit of disaggregation. The most obviously identifiable industry is nonmanufacturing; the obvious heterogeneity and large size of this industry make it undesirable that this be treated as one agent, but the limitations of the available data make this inevitable. Within manufacturing, the basic unit for an industry is a SIC order, with the exception that very small orders (those with a weight of less than 50—about two and a half percent of the total) are aggregated with the most appropriate large order. This produces nine manufacturing industries. These all appear reasonably homogeneous, with the exceptions of one containing orders VII (shipbuilding and marine engineering) and IX (metal goods not elsewhere specified), and one containing orders XIII (bricks, pottery, glass, cement, et cetera), XIV (timber, furniture, et cetera), and XVI (other manufacturing industries). The former is retained because together with orders VI (engineering and electrical goods) and VIII (vehicles), it comprises a larger SIC grouping (engineering and allied industries) for which only aggregate data is frequently given; the latter is a necessary residual which merely enlarges the SIC residual.

The detailed specification of the producing agents is given in

Table 3-1; this also provides a comparison of the basic 1958 SIC orders with other classifications which are used, and an identifying symbol. To avoid confusion with variables, these symbols (lowercase Latin letters) are always bold. Aggregation of industries is denoted by the adjunction of their symbols (for example the combination of industries **p** and **o** is denoted **po**). The symbol **I** designates the set of all primitive industries,

$$\mathbf{I} = \left\{ \mathbf{n, f, c, s, e, v, h, t, p, o} \right\} \quad,$$

while **M** and **C** refer to the sets of manufacturing and 'consumption' industries respectively,

$$\mathbf{M} = \mathbf{I} - \left\{ \mathbf{n} \right\}$$

$$\mathbf{C} = \left\{ \mathbf{f, v, t, o} \right\} \quad;$$

typical elements in these sets are denoted by **i** or **j**. For reference, these identifications are also given in Appendix A.

Table 3-1 also lists the aggregates **a** and **m**. This is because it is often more appropriate to give figures for these as well as for their components, for in some cases (where different sources have been used or where one source uses different methods) these aggregates are not the sum of their components; recording both makes any statistical discrepancy explicit.

Conventions

This preliminary discussion avoids repetition in the discussion of the individual series; however, there are a few exceptions to these general conventions, which are mentioned in context.

Variables (for example output, tax) are denoted by italic Latin letters (x, T); these symbols are given in the subheading introducing them, and are also reproduced in Appendix A. (It will become apparent in Chapter 4 that variables represented by lowercase letters are endogenous, and those represented by capital letters are exogenous.)

As far as possible all variables are expressed in their basic form, that is without seasonal adjustment and (where relevant) at current rather than base prices. This is because it is preferable to make any seasonal or inflation adjustment explicit—particularly since any such adjustment must be to some extent arbitrary. No mention is made of conversion from monthly source figures to quarterly figures unless this is of particular interest. All figures are given to the maximum number of decimal places that is meaningful, assuming that the sources do likewise. The first quarter of the year 1956 is referred to by the symbol 56.1, and so on.

Units are of course important; these are:

Table 3-1. Industry Classification

Symbol	Industry	Weight[1]	Order SIC 1958[2]	Order SIC 1948[3]	'The Economist'[4] Grouping	CDAE[5] Category
a	aggregate	1902[6]	I-XIII, XV-XXIII	I-XX, XXXIII, XXIV	total: all groups	1-31
m	manufacturing	748	III-XVI	III-XVI	sum of **M**	4-24
n	nonmanufacturing	1154[6]	I, II, XVII-XXIII	I, II, XVII, XX, XXIII, XXIV	a less m	1- 3 25-31
f	foods	86	III	XIII	breweries, etc.; food mfg.; tobacco	4, 5
c	chemicals	68	IV	IV	chemicals, etc.	6- 8
s	steel	68	V	V	iron and steel	9-11
e	engineering	167	VI	with h: VI, VIII, IX	electrical, etc.; engineering	12
v	vehicles	79	VIII	VII	motors, etc.	14-16
h	household	64	VII, IX	with e: VI, VIII, IX	shipbuilding; household, etc.	13, 17
t	textiles	92	X-XII	X-XII	textiles; clothing, etc.	18, 19
p	papers	55	XV	XV	paper, etc.; publishing, etc.	23
o	other	70	XIII, XIV, XVI	III, XIV, XVI	building, etc.; miscellaneous	20, 21 22, 24

Notes:
[1] See CSO [3].
[2] See CSO [2].
[3] See CSO [1].
[4] See *The Economist*.
[5] See CDAE [1].
[6] See Section 3.4.

1. Money flow variables are in millions of pounds per quarter
2. Stock variables are in millions of pounds or thousands of persons, as appropriate, at the end of the quarter
3. Rates (such as tax rates) are expressed as proportions
4. Indices (such as those of prices) are based so that the average over the decade 1956 to 1965 is unity.

Published sources are used predominantly, and in the few cases where unpublished material has to be used the original figures from this material are given in full in the text; thus duplication of all series is possible.

The main published sources are the *Monthly Digest of Statistics (MDS)* and *National Income and Expenditure (NIE)*; frequent reference is made to these in their abbreviated form followed by a number referring to the relevant table number in the (last) copy for the year following the observation period, that is the December 1967 *MDS* and the 1967 *NIE* . Within this limit, in all cases where these and other periodicals are used, the most recently published figures are taken. Further details of published series are frequently given in the table from which they originate or in the text, appendix, or supplement of the source; in general no such references are made, but should be inferred.

3.2 PRODUCERS VARIABLES

The individual variables representing the actions of the various producing agents, or industries, are now discussed.

Output (x)

Figures are quantum indices of gross output discussed in detail by CSO[3]; these are the only readily available figures. Possibly superior approximations to indices of net output may be derived from the component changes in gross output weighted in terms of some base period's net output, but this is not attempted. Gross output is relevant to production decision equations, but can only act as a proxy for net output, or value added, in production functions. The basic figures are from *MDS* 46, aggregated where necessary at the published weights. The published figures up to 58.3 are based on 1954, and since 58.3 on 1958; the two series are spliced by regressing the old series on the new for the available overlap period (ten quarters). This applies only to industry **m** and to **M**; figures for government are obtained by interpolating annual figures of gross national product attributable to government (that is public administration and defense, and public health and educational services—from *NIE* 11, deflated by the deflator of gross domestic product implicit in *MDS* 1) according to quarterly figures for government wages (see below). Gross domestic product (from *MDS* 2) is used for **a** plus government, the other aggregates being obtained from these by subtraction—**m** being weighted by the value of its contribution to gross national product in the base year 1958, from *NIE* 11.

Labor (l)

These are numbers of male and female, part time and full time, employees in Great Britain (GB), that is UK less Northern Ireland (as figures for the UK are not readily available); they apply to the middle of the quarter and are taken from *MDS* 14. Figures for **a** are those for the total in civil employment, less national and local government service. Various changes occur during the time period. In 59.2 the basic changes from SIC 1948 to SIC

1958; this is allowed for by adjusting the earlier figures by the ratio of the figures of the two classifications for this quarter (no longer overlap is available). Further, under the SIC 1948 industries **e** and **h** are aggregated; these are separated according to figures from the *Ministry of Labour Gazette*, the source of the *MDS* figures. The published figures are again revised in 64.3, earlier observations being adjusted according to the ratio in that quarter. The fact that all figures before 62.3 are taken two thirds of the way through the quarter is ignored. The last year of the observation period again involves a change, and figures for this year are taken from the *Ministry of Labour Gazette*, table 103 (**m** and for **M**), and *Statistics on Incomes, Prices, Employment and Production*, table E 1 (**a** and government). Throughout, figures for **n** are obtained by subtraction.

It should be emphasized that 'labor' is used throughout to refer to those actually employed—as opposed to 'labor force,' which includes those unemployed.

Unemployment (*u*)

Figures for unemployment are similar to those for labor, and again apply to GB; they originate from the *Ministry of Labour Gazette* 'Industrial Analysis of Unemployment' table; they are the total of males and females wholly and temporarily unemployed. In this case figures for the UK are available but are discarded in favor of those for GB to maintain consistency with the labor figures. The change from SIC 1948 to SIC 1958 in 59.3 is treated analogously to the change for labor, using the labor ratio as none is available for unemployment. Again figures for industries **m** (until 60.1) and **n** are obtained from the others.

Investment (*i*)

Figures are of gross fixed investment in all types of assets, and are taken almost directly from *MDS* 8. Industries **e** and **h**, which are combined in the source, are separated according to their relative proportions in each year (from *NIE* 60). Figures for industry **a** and for government are from *MDS* 7, the public corporation element of the figure for government before 64.1 being deducted according to the relative proportions of public corporations and public authorities in the total (from *NIE* 54)—this gives, as a check, reasonable figures for the period since 64.1. Industry **n** is again a residual.

It may be noted that *MDS* 8 gives extremely high figures for the year 1956, the total for which exceeds the corresponding figure given by *NIE* 60—by 74 percent. It is usual to expect some error in quarterly figures, especially for relatively volatile series such as investment, but this appears excessive. Accordingly, all figures for 1956 are divided by this factor (1.74) after allowing for the 'normal discrepancy'—taken as that for the year 1957.

Stocks (s)

These are total inventory stocks (materials and fuel, work in progress, and finished goods). The series are derived from figures for a base date and changes, sometimes as the value of physical increase and sometimes as the increase in book value, for preceding and subsequent quarters. Figures for the period up to 59.4 are obtained by subtracting cumulatively the change in value of stocks at current prices for each quarter from the value of stocks held at the end of 59.4; all figures are from *MDS* 6 except those for industry a (from *MDS* 2), the figures for s plus evh and for c plus po being separated according to their ratios at the end of 59.4. After 59.4 the process is rather more complex: the values of the physical increase in each quarter at current prices are deflated by the relevant price indices, to give figures for the values of physical increase at constant (1958) prices (though in fact these are given directly at 1958 prices until 62.4), which are then added cumulatively to the value of stocks held, at 1958 prices, at the end of 59.4. The resulting figures of stocks held at 1958 prices are then reflated by the same price indices to give stocks held at current prices. This gives figures for industries a and m, and for M (though no attempt is made to separate industries evh and po). Figures for government for the whole period are obtained by subtracting cumulatively the increase in book value of stocks by year from their value at the end of 1966, both at current prices (from *NIE* 71), to give figures for the fourth quarters, and linearly interpolating to give figures for the first, second, and third quarters in each year. Figures for industry n are then obtained by subtraction.

The price indices used are weighted averages of the input and output prices for each industry. The weights are: for input prices, the value of materials and fuel held plus (an arbitrary) half of the value of work in progress at the end of 59.4, and for output prices, the value of finished products plus half of the value of work in progress at the same date—both expressed as proportions of the total; however, for industry s arbitrary weights of a half each are taken because of lack of data. Ideally, the three types of inventory asset should be treated separately but this is not attempted. Where there is no exactly-corresponding wholesale price the assumed next best is used; these series, together with the weights, are given in Table 3–2 (industry n and government do not appear, since their series are not adjusted by price indices).

Price (p)

Figures are indices of the ex works prices of output, and exclude any purchase taxes, though include excise duty. They cover industries m, f, c, s, t, p, and a residual evho, and are from *MDS* 167. The series for industry m, which covers home market sales only, is given in a revised form from 63.1, so the earlier part of the series is adjusted according to a regression of the new series on the old over the overlap period of eight quarters. Figures for the

Table 3-2. Stock Deflators

Industry	Series Used		Weights	
	Input Price	*Output Price*	*Input Price*	*Output Price*
a	m	m	0.500	0.500
m	m	m	0.532	0.468
f	f	f	0.580	0.420
c	c	c	0.516	0.484
s	e	s	0.607	0.393
evh	e	s	0.526	0.474
t	t	t	0.476	0.524
po	p	p	0.510	0.490

residual industry and industry **t** (from 'textile industries other than clothing' and 'clothing and footwear') are weighted averages, the weights being those of the index of production. As no quarterly figures are available for 1956, the annual figure is taken for all quarters. No figures at all are available for industry **n** (later the price for **n** will be taken to be that for **m**, but this is an aspect of the model rather than of the data).

Earnings (e)

These are average quarterly earnings of all employees, male and female, wage and salary receiving, expressed in thousands of pounds (so that earnings multiplied by labor produces labor income in millions of pounds). The figures are derived in three main stages. Firstly, figures of average weekly earnings for adult men manual workers in the second pay week of April and October each year (as published in the *Ministry of Labour Gazette* statistical series, table 122 [December 1967]) are assigned to the second and fourth quarters of each year. Until 59.4 these figures are based on the 1948 SIC and industries **e** and **h** are combined; allowance is made for the change from the 1948 to the 1958 SIC by adjusting the earlier series by the ratio of the figures for the two classifications for 59.4, and industries **e** and **h** are separated according to their (almost equal) means over the rest of the period. Secondly, figures of average earnings of all employees for all quarters from 63.1 are taken from the *Ministry of Labour Gazette* statistical series, table 127 [December 1967], and the figures from the first stage are regressed on these for each second and fourth quarter from 63.2 onwards, and are adjusted accordingly. Figures for the first and third quarters before 63.1 are then derived by interpolating the second and fourth quarter figures according to the mean seasonal from 63.1 on, so

$$e_\tau^3 = e_\tau^2 + (e_\tau^4 - e_\tau^2) \sum_\tau (e_\tau^3 - e_\tau^2) / \sum_\tau (e_\tau^4 - e_\tau^2) \ ,$$

$$e_\tau^1 = e_{\tau-1}^4 + (e_\tau^2 - e_{\tau-1}^4) \sum_\tau (e_\tau^1 - e_{\tau-1}^4) / \sum_\tau (e_\tau^2 - e_{\tau-1}^4),$$

where e_τ^σ is earnings in $\tau \cdot \sigma$ (that is quarter σ of year τ), and the summation operator is over the years 1963 to 1966. This process effectively maintains the same seasonal throughout the series, rather than introducing possible distortions by incorporating a different seasonal in the first part of the series—where the difference is entirely attributable to the interpolating process. Thirdly, the series from the second stage are used to interpolate annual figures of total wages and salaries (form *NIE* 18 for m and M, *NIE* 17 for a) divided by the number of employees (same source for m and M, see labor series for a) to give average quarterly earnings. Finally, figures for n are obtained as the weighted (by labor) difference between a and m.

Three points deserve mention here. Firstly, the desirability of dividing aggregate earnings into (at least) wage earnings and salary earnings becomes apparent; it can be partially countered by the need for simplicity and by the closeness of the two series. This is illustrated in the *Ministry of Labour Gazette* [December 1967], which shows salaries (earnings or rates—approximately equivalent), weekly wage earnings, and weekly wage rates over the period: there are marked differences between salaries and wage rates, but salaries and wage earnings follow an almost identical path, which suggests that it may be acceptable to combine the two. Secondly, further insight may be obtainable at the cost of greater complexity by dividing earnings in another dimension, into hourly earnings and average hours; this again is omitted mainly for simplicity—the point is further discussed in Chapter 4. Thirdly, the final series have been obtained in a rather circumspect way, which includes the splicing of series for men manual workers with those for all workers. However, the resulting series is only used to interpolate an annual series, and in fact the degree of correlation between the two spliced series is high: in only one industry (v, where it is 0·90) is the squared correlation coefficient (for eight observations) less than 0·95.

Profits (z)

These are gross trading profits of companies operating in the UK; they exclude (or are measured before provision for) depreciation, stock appreciation, tax, interest payments, investment and rental income, and net income derived from abroad—that is they are the reward of fixed factors for domestic production. The basic figures are those published in *The Economist* 'Industrial Profits and Assets' series; these give trading profits of companies, disaggregated into twenty-three industries, reporting in each quarter—both for the latest year and for the previous year for the same companies. These are combined into a continuous series by a method suggested by Prais, which comprises three main stages. Firstly, a lag of two quarters is introduced to allow (rather arbitrarily) for the delay between the earning and the reporting of profits. Secondly, the figures are partially aggregated to conform to the SIC classification of industries, and for each industry for each quarter linked series are derived showing the year to year movements in profits for the companies reporting in each quarter. This gives four series of indices for each industry, and as the ratios from year to year for each quarterly series are the ratios of the latest to previous reported profits for the same companies, the change in the index depends solely on the true change in profits, not on the change in composition of the sample. Thirdly, these four independent series are combined into a single continuous series by what Prais [p. 7] calls 'a process which is almost exactly analagous to seasonal "adjustment" ': the mean annual trend for each quarterly series is calculated, together with the average of these four means, which is expressed as a quarterly figure. It is then assumed that the means of the four series should differ by this average proportional trend, and a correction factor is applied to each of the series (except that for the first quarter—taken as the base), so that this assumption is satisfied. The resulting continuous series is then used to interpolate annual figures of gross trading profits by industry (from *NIE* 35), to which is added, where appropriate (industries a and s), gross trading surplusses of public corporations (from *NIE* 39). (This is the one exception where final figures were not available by the end of 1967; figures for the year 1966 are from *NIE* for 1968.) Finally, this method is only applied to industry a and to **M**; figures for **m** and **n** are obtained directly from these.

Figures for profits are open to many objections, for more than most other variables they are in practice dependent on the frequently incompatible accounting conventions of individual firms. Disaggregation by industry and quarter increases the possible hazards and thus less confidence may be attached to figures for profits than to most other series. In particular, there are three main objections.

Firstly, figures ascribed to a quarter are not 'true' figures of profits generated in that quarter, but a four-quarter moving average centered on the quarter; thus the figures are in effect seasonally adjusted and open to the dangers of this, as mentioned above. There is, however, no way of improving the series for profits without new information, which is not available.

Secondly, the rate of growth of profits implied by the continuous series used to interpolate the annual data may be observed to be higher in nearly all cases than the rate of growth of the annual figures. This implies that *The Economist* sample is biased towards growth companies, which may be reasonable since its choice is restricted to public companies, which might be expected to grow more rapidly than the average. The implication of this is that the figures derived for the first and second quarters of each year might be expected to be too small, and for the third and fourth too large.

Thirdly, there is a basic objection to the use of a geometric linked series as suggested by Prais, that is where (in the notation used for earnings)

$$(\text{index})_T^g = (\text{index})_{T-1}^g \ (\text{latest profits})_T^g / (\text{previous profits})_T^g \ ,$$

when any profits figure is not strictly positive. For example it only requires one small loss (latest or previous) to turn all subsequent profits into losses, and a zero previous profit produces indeterminacy. This objection is of little practical importance where highly aggregated figures are used, but can become very relevant where small groups of volatile companies are examined: although only giving aggregate figures, Prais derives these from weighted averages of geometrically linked series for twenty industrial groups. Because of this the use of an arithmetically linked series, that is where

$$(\text{index})_T^g = (\text{index})_{T-1}^g + (\text{latest profits})_T^g$$

$$- (\text{previous profits})_T^g$$

(using a suitable base), or a weighted average of arithmetically and geometrically linked series, was considered. This would be justifiable conceptually if reported profits consist in part of planned remuneration to capital (interest) and in part of a residual (pure profit); the former might be expected to conform to a geometrically linked series indicating exponential growth while the latter might conform to an arithmetically linked one indicating the random nature of the residual element. This hypothesis may be tested for part of the data, as the linked series of profits reported in the second quarter of each year should reflect the actual profits of the previous calendar year. The correlation between the true series and both arithmetically and geometrically linked series is thus examined for each industry. The results are far from conclusive, but slightly favor a geometrically linked series, which, with one minor modification, is therefore used. This modification concerns industry h for 65.4, where the reported latest profit is negative; this observation is discarded, it being arbitrarily assumed that the proportional change for that period is the geometric mean of the proportional changes in the immediately preceding and subsequent periods.

Finally, a check of the whole procedure is possible for industry a, where estimates of true figures of (aggregate) quarterly profits are obtainable from *MDS* 2—with allowance for the change of status of the Post Office in 61.2. Comparing these derived and direct figures indicates that the procedure adopted is at least acceptable—for the aggregate, which is all that can be checked. The trends are the same (naturally, due to the interpolation process) and more importantly, the turning points in each series on the whole coincide; the main apparent difference is that the derived series fluctuates rather more violently, that is each peak and trough tends to be slightly exaggerated. There is no real evidence of the suggested underestimation of the first and second quarters and overestimation of the fourth. Of course such a test can only provide an indication of the acceptability of the procedure, but it is all that is available.

Capital (k)

Figures of gross fixed capital stock are based on data of the Cambridge Department of Applied Economics (CDAE) [3], an unpublished revision of the published figures of CDAE [2]; a condensed matrix of the original figures is given in Table 3-3. The figures provided are disaggregated by industry (twenty-one categories of manufacturing and ten of nonmanufacturing) and by type of asset (buildings, plant, and vehicles), and are at constant (1954) prices; their derivation is briefly summarized here.

The basic method assumes a life of, say, T periods for different types of asset (not necessarily the same in different industries), and figures for gross investment at constant prices, i, are obtained for each industry and asset over a period which is twice the life of each asset. Now all capital of a given type purchased in period τ ends its life, or is scrapped, in period $T + \tau$, so scrapping in period τ is $i_{\tau\text{-}T\text{-}1}$ and extensions to gross stock, that is gross investment less scrapping, is given by $i_\tau - i_{\tau\text{-}T\text{-}1}$. But extensions are merely a change of gross stock, or alternatively, gross stock is the sum of all extensions still existing, that is made over the past $T + 1$ periods. One has then

$$k_\tau = \sum_{\sigma=\tau-T-1}^{\tau} i_\sigma - i_{\sigma-T-1} .$$

Table 3-3. Capital Stocks

Year	f	c	s	e	Industry v	h	t	p	o
1955	1289.9	1172.3	1092.7	1674.1	989.1	608.1	2068.8	784.9	768.6
1956	1330.1	1283.0	1175.7	1749.9	1040.8	633.4	2077.5	820.3	810.6
1957	1377.3	1407.6	1266.1	1823.1	1090.7	660.8	2085.6	858.7	854.9
1958	1425.0	1528.5	1355.7	1893.4	1124.2	687.9	2079.8	887.9	897.4
1959	1467.7	1628.6	1434.8	1951.1	1153.2	721.9	2074.2	910.8	943.6
1960	1521.8	1713.8	1567.5	2032.4	1192.1	755.4	2085.0	942.3	1005.7
1961	1577.5	1816.5	1762.8	2121.9	1254.6	792.4	2104.1	976.3	1070.4
1962	1633.3	1913.9	1917.2	2200.7	1311.5	825.9	2112.4	1010.6	1137.2
1963	1695.8	1981.4	2000.7	2281.5	1364.9	852.7	2112.3	1042.6	1197.8
1964	1770.3	2076.6	2070.3	2374.3	1409.2	887.8	2143.7	1082.1	1272.7
1965	1856.5	2208.8	2136.5	2460.8	1479.1	922.3	2182.2	1129.8	1376.1
(see									
note)	91.3	40.7	22.1	67.2	21.3	21.1	40.6	23.7	74.6

Note:
The last row gives figures for vehicles for 1965 computed as described in the text; these are included in the figures in the main table, for the source only gives figures for buildings and plant for that year. A figure of 470.7 is similarly included for buildings in industry o for 1965.

The treatment of this basic data has four main stages. Firstly, as the figures provided end in 1965, and in some cases in 1964, the series are brought up to date using the method described above; figures for gross investment for each industry and asset at 1954 prices are obtained by deflating current price figures for investment from *NIE* by the price deflators implicit in *NIE* 54. Investment T (Table 3-4) years before is frequently unavailable, and so it is assumed that scrapping remains at its preceding year's level (Table 3-4)—the stability of scrapping in the CDAE figures over the last few years suggests that this is not unrealistic. Secondly, all figures are expressed in terms of the average price level over the decade 1956 to 1965, rather than in terms of the 1954 price level; this is to maintain consistency, and has little importance since it involves only multiplying by a scalar, derived from figures provided by the source and given in Table 3-4. (This is an exception to the general convention of using current prices, and is made partly because constant price values for capital stock are of particular relevance, but mainly because in this isolated case the primary figures are at constant prices so there is no question of introducing, just of inevitably retaining, possibly arbitrary deflators.) Thirdly, industries (where necessary) and asset types are aggregated; ideally it would be preferable to keep the types of asset separate, but this is not attempted. Fourthly, the resulting figures are allocated to the fourth quarters of each year, and these are linearly interpolated to produce figures for the first, second, and third quarters.

This procedure only gives data for **M**, from which figures for **m** are obtained; figures for **a** are based on those of total gross capital stock (excluding private dwellings, public dwellings, roads, and other public social services) from *NIE* 66, given for the years 1954, 1958, and 1961 to 1966—intermediate observations are derived from linear interpolation. Similar *NIE* figures for **m** were also derived, but these, after conversion to 1954 prices, showed marked differences from the processed CDAE figures: accordingly, the *NIE* figures

Table 3-4. Capital Scrapping

Industry	Latest Scrapping			Life (Years)		
	Buildings	*Plant*	*Vehicles*	*Buildings*	*Plant*	*Vehicles*
f	13.3	18.6	15.6	50.0	27.5	7.0
c	3.3	20.6	5.2	50.0	27.0	7.0
s	4.5	20.1	3.0	50.0	17.0	7.0
e	10.1	33.0	9.1	50.0	27.5	7.0
v	7.3	11.3	1.4	50.0	24.4	7.0
h	4.7	17.0	3.9	50.0	24.3	7.0
t	22.5	38.9	7.2	50.0	28.0	7.0
p	6.2	16.4	3.9	50.0	27.6	7.0
o	6.2	9.2	9.9	50.0	27.3	7.0

Price Reflators: Buildings, 1.220; Plant, 1.253; Vehicles, 1.056.

for **a** are multiplied by the ratio of the CDAE estimates for **m** to the equivalent *NIE* figures. No obvious reason for the discrepancy is apparent; the *NIE* figures are made compatible with the CDAE figures, rather than vice versa, purely for convenience, since there is no immediately available basis for assessing their relative accuracies. This is of minor importance since the ratio between the two sets of figures remains relatively stable. Figures for **n** are obtained by subtraction.

3.3 CONSUMERS VARIABLES

The discussion now turns to those variables which, for convenience (and in some cases only because they are naturally identified with no industry), are associated with the final, or consumer, agent.

Consumption (c)

Figures for consumers' expenditure (and other series relating to this—consumer prices and tax rates) are divided into four categories: food, drink, and tobacco (corresponding approximately to the final output of industry **f** and identified accordingly), motor vehicles (**v**), clothing and footwear (**t**), and other (**o**). The essence of this disaggregation is the removal of three relatively homogeneous and easily defined groups from the whole, rather than the definition of four meaningful categories—hence the large residual. All figures are from *MDS* 5, those for category **o** being derived by subtraction.

Consumer Prices (b)

Indices of consumer prices for the relevant categories are from *MDS* 165, aggregated where necessary at the published weights. From 62.1 the published figures are (annually) linked indices, and before this they are based on January 1956; the earlier figures are therefore adjusted according to the ratio of the new series to the old in January 1962 (no longer overlap being available). Category **v** is from the disaggregated figures of *MDS* 166, subgroup 'motoring and cycling.'

Exports (n)

Figures for exports (and other trade series—imports and world trade) are obtained for the aggregate, **a**, and the two main divisions of this, **n** and **m**. They represent the value of UK produce exported, measured free-on-board; figures are obtained from *MDS* 129, **a** directly, **m** by addition, and **n** by subtraction.

Imports (m)

Imports, valued to include cost, insurance, and freight, are obtained in the same way as exports, from *MDS* 129.

World Trade (Q)

Figures are quantum indices of world exports excluding Mainland China, Russia, and Eastern Europe; they are from the *Monthly Bulletin of Statistics* Table 'Selected Series of World Statistics.' In 61.2 the base changes from 1954 to 1958 and, as no overlap of quarterly figures is available, the series are spliced according to a regression of the old annual figures on the new over four years. Figures for n are weighted differences of figures for a and m, the weights being the values of these categories in 1958, obtained from the *Statistical Yearbook* Summary Table 12 [1966 issue].

Income Tax (T)

This is the average rate of tax on all income from employment. Like the profit and consumption tax rates, it is an annual figure allocated to all quarters. This may possibly cause distortion from the true proportion as rates are usually altered near the end of the first quarter; distortion may also arise due to the fact that no account can readily be taken of the lag between the receipt of income (or consumption) and the payment of tax—though this might be expected to be of greatest relevance to the series for profit tax rates.

The income tax rate series is obtained by dividing income tax and surtax (after 1962 allocated according to the breakdown in that year) charged on all income from employment (from *NIE* 51) by the total income from employment (*NIE* 1).

Profit Tax (R)

This is the average rate of tax on corporate income, obtained by dividing taxes on the income of companies and public corporations (from *NIE* 51) by total gross trading profits (or surplusses) of companies and public corporations (*NIE* 1). Again this is an annual rate allocated to all quarters.

Consumption Tax (D)

Figures are annual proportions of consumers' expenditure absorbed by all forms of indirect taxation, and apply to the four consumption categories. They are derived by dividing annual figures for taxes on consumers' expenditure (from *NIE* 29) by the corresponding figures for consumption (*NIE* 27). No allowance is made for expenditure by foreign tourists in the UK or consumers' expenditure abroad.

Government Goods (F)

This is total purchases on current account of goods and services (excluding direct labor but including other factor costs such as imputed rents) by government; it is obtained by subtracting government wages from total public authorities current expenditure (from *MDS* 1).

Government Wages (*W*)

This is total direct expenditure on current account on wages and salaries by government, excluding wages and salaries paid in trading services; figures are obtained by interpolating an annual series (from *NIE* 48) according to the series of total public authorities current expenditure, from *MDS* 1.

Government Transfers (*V*)

This is total current grants from public authorities from *MDS* 4; it consists of national insurance benefits, family allowances, assistance grants, and so forth (but excludes government interest payments).

Government Investment (*J*)

This is total expenditure on capital account, that is gross fixed investment plus the change in the value of stocks held, by government; it is obtained by adding the series derived for investment for government to the first difference of that derived for stocks for government.

3.4 MISCELLANEOUS CONSTANTS

The necessary time series data to represent producers' and consumers' actions are now available. However, some further information is needed: not time series data, but certain established constants. Strictly speaking, these constitute parts of the numerical specification of the model rather than the data; however, they are discussed here for convenience. The constants themselves are given in Appendix B.

There are three sets of such constants—the first two of rather nominal, but the third of more real, importance. These are weights, bases, and input-output coefficients; they are represented by lowercase Greek symbols, superscripted (once or twice, as appropriate) by industry.

Weights (*ν*)

These reflect the relative sizes of the ten industries; they are basically the (1958) weights in the index of industrial production given by CSO [3] and listed in Table 3-1. This does not produce a weight for industry n; the weight for this industry is obtained from its contribution to gross domestic product in 1958 from *NIE* 11:

$$\nu^n = \nu^m \pi^n / \pi^m \ ,$$

where ν^i is the weight for, and π^i the product originating in, industry i

($i = m, n$). These figures, expressed as proportions so that their sum is unity, form the elements of the vector $[\nu^i]$, $i \in I$.

Bases (μ)

These are the bases of the series of value of output, that is output multiplied by price. These series are both weighted for the year 1958, and accordingly the bases are calculated for that year. The base for each industry is obtained by dividing the value originating in terms of labor income (labor multiplied by earnings) plus profits, by the index of value originating in terms of (average for the year) output multiplied by price. This process gives the vector $[\mu^i]$, $i \in I$.

Input-Output (λ)

The input-output matrix (λ^{ij}), $i, j \in I$, is derived from CDAE [1]. Each element, λ^{ij}, of this matrix gives the direct demand for the output of industry i by industry j per unit output of industry j for the year 1960, at 1960 prices.

Ideally, a matrix typical of the observation period is required. To achieve this, some form of average matrix might be constructed, for example by making each element equal to the mean of the corresponding elements in matrices for each of the years of the time period, such matrices being derived from any two base matrices by the 'RAS' method proposed by CDAE [1]. This is not attempted because (estimated) data for a year almost in the middle of the time period, 1960, is readily available.

Simple input-output matrices are based on a homogeneity assumption, that is they assume that there is a one-to-one mapping from the set of industries into that of commodities, so that the make matrix is diagonal. More sophisticated analyses accept the nondiagonality of the make matrix, but make another less restricting assumption: either, in the terminology of CDAE [1], that *'all commodities, whether principal or subsidiary, produced in one industry are made by the same process and therefore require the same input structure'* [p. 13] —the industry technology; or that 'technological processes depend on the nature of the individual commodities produced, and therefore that *inputs are determined not by the industry which absorbs them but by the commodity into which they enter'* [p. 14] —the commodity technology. The environment in which the matrix is to be used dictates the use of the most simple (homogeneity) assumption; as the CDAE matrix is based on the commodity technology it is adjusted accordingly.

The first part of this process makes the two disaggregation schemes compatible by condensing the CDAE make matrix [Table 5] and absorption matrix [Table 6] for 1960 at 1960 prices from order thirty-one to order ten. The validity of the homogeneity hypothesis at this level of disaggregation may be investigated by examining the nonzero offdiagonal elements in the condensed make matrix. It transpires that the offdiagonal elements are of relatively little importance in all industries, and the sum of all offdiagonal elements (which involves no cancelling) is only approximately 2.7 percent of the sum of all elements. Reasonable confidence may thus be attached to the homogeneity assumption.

If the validity of the homogeneity hypothesis is accepted, an input-output matrix is readily derived from an absorption matrix by dividing each element in the latter by the total output of the relevant purchasing industry (or the total output of the commodity produced by that industry). Thus the condensed absorption matrix is treated in this way, a simple average of the total output of the relevant industry and commodity being used as the divisor.

Chapter Four

Theoretical Model

One must now specify, as fully as possible, an action rule for each of the eleven agents (the ten producers and one consumer). As this must be an a priori, or theoretical, specification, it cannot be expected to be complete; it must however be of sufficient detail to allow its completion from a coincidental examination of it and the data. The chapter commences with a discussion of the general approach, then considers models for the various agents—producers' then consumer's.

4.1 GENERAL APPROACH

Since this study is one of interaction, it is profitable to suggest a (loose) framework in which agents are able to interact before specifying in detail the ways in which they affect each other.

Basic Method

As was seen in Part I, the agent's action rule is defined by the maximization of his preference ordering over his choice set. Conceptually then, all one need do is specify this preference relation and choice set. In practice, however, it turns out to be more helpful to proceed less directly: to specify an action rule which appears more arbitrary, but which is based implicitly rather than explicitly on this framework. This is the standard method of attack in empirical models, and one which is followed here.

The implicit preference ordering for producers is naturally related to profit, but need not be profit in its narrowly defined sense; this relaxation of the theory may be justified by the whole established literature on 'behavioral' models of the firm. The choice set for producers is even less clear: it is of course related to the physical production set, but the whole 'institutional' arrangements of the economy make other factors relevant. The 'consumer,' as noted, is really much more than a consumer, which naturally blurs any definition of his preference ordering and choice set. Even for the consumer proper, where the basic concepts would be a preference relation over the commodity space and a budget constraint, things may not be so simple: one may recognize (respectively) money illusion or imperfect borrowing facilities.

The main purpose then of this chapter is not to attempt to delve more deeply into the theoretical foundations of econometric models, but rather to turn the established empirical micro-framework into an empirical general equilibrium analysis. Although there is no comparison of the advances made, there is a methodological parallel to such seminal purely theoretical analyses as those of Marx or von Neumann, which used much more naive micro-foundations than were available to construct most valuable general equilibrium models.

Since all producers' models originate in the framework of profit maximization over a production set one should expect to find some basic core common to all such models. Equivalently, one should only expect these models to differ because of the physical nature of the product (defining the production set) and the 'effectiveness' of the producer (in maximizing his profit). The former concept is clear, but not the latter: since agents are in fact many individuals, what is meant by effectiveness is essentially their ability to act as a group, or in other words the degree of competition of their industry.

The approach will be that of specifying a 'standard' model to apply, with the appropriately different numerical parameters, to all the producing agents, or industries. The consumer's model will of course be basically different, since it originates from different preference relations and choice sets.

Values

One of the first general questions to consider is whether to work in current or deflated values. The emphasis (for producers) on the profit maximizing rationale suggests that the more usual approach of working primarily in deflated values may be inappropriate: partly because of the high dependence of profits on prices, and partly because of the conceptual difficulties involved in deflating profits. For example, this may be illustrated by Evans' study of profits, which finds that using money values rather than real values in equations for profits in twenty-one industries explains on average an additional eighteen percent of the residual variance, and concludes [p. 356] that 'current dollar values are far superior to constant dollar values in explaining profits.'

There are three basic ways (which may be mixed) of treating this question. Firstly, and conceptually preferable, is the fullest treatment where all variables are expressed in both value and volume terms. This requires a large number of equations, including a price adjustment equation for each variable, often with associated inventory holding functions, and the indentity that value is equal to volume multiplied by price. Naturally, it causes severe practical difficulties in disaggregated models.

Secondly, money values may be used. This is clearly inappropriate for purely technical relationships such as production functions, but is perhaps more appropriate than is sometimes supposed for many decision equations. It is observable that there is some money illusion, especially in the short run: if the pound is the standard unit of account than both producers and consumers will tend to base their decisions on pounds, rather than on '1958 pounds.' This is desirable, for the pound is a meaningfully defined unit whereas the '1958 pound' is not; the conceptual problems of defining meaningful price indices, particularly where there are quality changes and new goods, are well known. This applies to flows of measurable quantities of goods and services; for residuals and other nonflow variables the problems are greater, and of course at the practical level they are greater still for both categories. The use of money variables in demand functions may be criticized on the grounds that it is not consistent with the supposition that such functions are homogeneous of degree zero in prices. Apart from the question of whether this requirement should theoretically be fulfilled in the short run (and by accepting some money illusion it is suggested that it need not), this may be unimportant in practice for linear equations whose values cover a small range, for the nonhomogeneous linear relation may be interpreted as an approximation to a nonlinear relation that is homogeneous.

Thirdly, there is the (usual) practice of using deflated values. The main problem with this is its treatment of the usual accounting identites, which strictly apply only to money relationships and not to deflated values. An example, observed by Christ [1], of the dangers of working with deflated variables appears in the well-known model of Klein and Goldberger. In this model consumption is deflated by a price index for consumer goods, while disposable income is deflated by an index for gross national product. As the latter increased relative to the former over the observation period, though only by about eight percent over twenty-three years, the model gives deflated disposable income a downward bias relative to consumption. Thus serious errors in the predicted values of personal saving, obtained from the identity between the three variables, are produced—by making the identity apply to deflated values. Saving then is too high at the beginning of the period and too low at the end, even becoming negative in one year. This sort of result from a mild change of relative prices strengthens the case for the use of money values.

If practical considerations rule out the first more detailed approach, the next best would seem to be the use of deflated values for purely physical relations, and of current values for behavioral relations. This is the approach adopted.

Seasonals
A second general problem in a quarterly model is the treatment of seasonal effects. There are essentially two methods of doing this: (explicit) adjustment of variables, and (implicit) adjustment of relations.

The former uses one of the standard nonparametric methods to deseasonalize all variables, and then works with these variables. However, it is well known that such methods (typically comparison with seasonally similar periods, and moving averages) suffer from serious statistical deficiencies—most notably, though not exclusively, autocorrelation.

Because of these problems the second method is adopted. This introduces three dummy variables, say *A, B,* and *C* (not related to the *a, b, c* used in Chapter 3) which have a value of unity in the first, second, and third quarters of the year respectively, otherwise being zero. Implicit in this is a fourth dummy which is always zero, which achieves the convention of treating the fourth quarter's value as the true value. Thus if one required to estimate the deseasonalized parameters (α_1, α_2) of the linear stochastic relation

$$y = \alpha_1 + \alpha_2 x + \omega \ ,$$

where *x, y,* and ω are, respectively, the independent variable, dependent variable, and stochastic residual, one would simply estimate the parameters $(\beta_1, \ldots \beta_5)$ of the equation

$$y = \beta_1 + \beta_2 A + \beta_3 B + \beta_4 C + \beta_5 x + \omega' \ .$$

This approach has the advantage of showing the depletion in the number of degrees of freedom (that is three), and allowing the valid use of normal methods of statistical inference. It does however depend on the assumption that the seasonal effects are additive and linear. This could be overcome at the cost of greater complexity, but the simple hypothesis is retained as a reasonable approximation. Of course this method does not directly produce information on the seasonal variation of each variable, but on the variation in each equation, where it is an aggregate of the variations of each variable in the equation. Seasonal adjustment of variables themselves could be achieved by estimating the parameters of the above equation without the *x* term, but this is not relevant here.

Distributed Lags
The model makes much use of hypotheses concerning the expected values (not in the statistical sense) and desired values of variables, which are most conveniently explained in terms of distributed lags. To avoid repetition, this digression briefly reviews two relevant interpretations of such Koyck transforms; though not of direct relevance at this stage, some statistical implications are, for convenience, also mentioned here.

Assume that there are two variables, *x* and *y*, such that *y* is an exact linear function of the expected value of *x*, say *x**, so

$$y = \alpha + \beta x^*$$

where α and β are constants. Further assume that the expected value of a variable, x^*, is a weighted average of its actual value, x, and the expected value held in the preceding period, say x^*_{-1}, (that is of the last expectation and its materialization) so that

$$x^* = \gamma x + (1 - \gamma)x^*_{-1}$$

where $\gamma \in [0, 1]$ is a constant; if γ is zero the present expectation is merely the last expectation, if it is unity it is simply the actual value. Substituting gives

$$y = \alpha + \beta\gamma x + \beta(1 - \gamma)x^*_{-1} \ ,$$

or

$$y = \alpha\gamma + \beta\gamma x + (1 - \gamma) \, y_{-1} \ .$$

Alternatively, one may assume that the desired level of y, say y^0, is an exact linear function of x, so

$$y^0 = \alpha + \beta x \ ,$$

and that the adjustment of y to its desired level is imperfect, only a fraction $\gamma \in [0, 1]$ of the difference between the desired and actual levels being made up in a period, that is

$$y - y_{-1} = \gamma(y - y_{-1}) \ .$$

Substituting gives

$$y = \alpha\gamma + \beta\gamma x + (1 - \gamma)y_{-1} \ ,$$

just as in the expected value case. Thus these exact hypotheses using expected and desired values are equivalent.

Now assume that y is a linear function of the expected value of x and a random disturbance, ω, so that

$$y = \alpha + \beta x^* + \omega \ ;$$

further, assume the same type of expectations hypothesis, though now involving a disturbance, ν, so that

$$x^* = \gamma x + (1 - \gamma)x_{-1}^* + v \ .$$

This gives

$$y = \alpha\gamma + \beta\gamma x + (1 - \gamma)y_{-1} + (\omega + \beta v - (1 - \gamma)\omega_{-1}) \ ,$$

which is equivalent to the exact case plus a (composite) disturbance term. However, the disturbance term is of interest, for it will in general be serially correlated even if the two original disturbances are not, since it includes the term $\omega - (1 - \gamma)\omega_{-1}$, which is correlated with its previous value, $\omega_{-1} - (1 - \gamma)\omega_{-2}$, since both contain ω_{-1} (unless $\gamma = 1$). Thus, estimation of the transformed equation is more complicated than that of the original equation if the latter is free from serial correlation. If this already has positive serial correlation, which is relatively common in economics, estimation of the transformed equation may be simpler than that of the original equation. If the ω are serially correlated with a first order autoregression coefficient of $1 - \gamma$, so that

$$\omega = (1 - \gamma)\omega_{-1} + \eta$$

where η is a (serially independent) disturbance term, then $\omega - (1 - \gamma)\omega_{-1}$ is serially independent; this of course is unlikely, but the commonness of positive serial correlation (that is $1 - \gamma > 0$) suggests that this transform may well reduce serial correlation.

It is important to note that the transformed equation includes y_{-1} as an explanatory variable, which raises further possible complications. If y is serially correlated so that y_{-1} is related to y then y_{-1} is not truly predetermined, and treating it as such may introduce simultaneous equation bias. This is a matter of more general relevance, and is mentioned in Chapter 5.

Alternatively, one may assume an equivalent stochastic desired value, or imperfect adjustment hypothesis, so that

$$y^0 = \alpha + \beta x + \omega$$

and

$$y - y_{-1} = \gamma(y^0 - y_{-1}) + v \ ,$$

which yields

$$y = \alpha\gamma + \beta\gamma x + (1 - \gamma)y_{-1} + (\gamma\omega + v) \ .$$

This is equivalent to the corresponding exact case plus a disturbance term, but is not equivalent to the expected value case—since the disturbance term here does not introduce any serial correlation. Neither model alters the nature of the distribution of the disturbance term, for if, as is assumed, these independently are normal, then any linear combination of them is also normal.

These are the two observationally equivalent transformations of this type used in the model. They may be shown to be two particular interpretations of the general distributed lag hypothesis that y is a function of x and all previous values (here in discrete time) of x, such that the coefficients of lagged values are geometrically declining, that is

$$y = \alpha + \beta_0 x + \beta_1 x_{-1} + \ldots$$

where $\beta_i = \rho\beta_{i-1}$ and $\rho \in [0, 1]$ is a constant. Then

$$y = \alpha + \beta_0 \sum_{i=0}^{\infty} \rho^i x_{-i} \ ,$$

so

$$y_{-1} = \alpha + (\beta_0/\rho) \sum_{i=0}^{\infty} \rho^{i+1} x_{-(i+1)} \ ,$$

$$= \alpha + (\beta_0/\rho) \sum_{i=1}^{\infty} (\rho^i x_{-1}) \ ,$$

so subtraction gives

$$y = \alpha(1 - \rho) + \beta_0 x + \rho y_{-i} \ ,$$

which is equivalent to both the expected value and the desired value hypotheses—if ρ is replaced by $1 - \gamma$.

Industry Outline
The 'standard' outline model which is proposed for each industry consists of ten equations, and thus involves ten endogenous variables. It also contains other (linking) variables which are endogenous to the complete model yet exogenous to the individual industry, and various purely exogenous and predetermined variables. Since profit determination is the basis of the industry models, an alternative to the standard formulation of profit is also considered, parenthetically (it is later shown that this is not helpful—in Chapter 6).

It is desirable to consider one variable or combination of variables as being dependent in each equation of the model, and thus as being determined explicitly. The equations of the outline model are thus chosen with the intention of forming a logically plausible whole before any attention is given to the detailed specification.

The first of these equations expresses the demand for the industry's output in value terms as the sum of the individual demands; parallel to this is a technological supply relation giving physical output as a function of factor inputs. Tying these two together is the important short-term relationship determining the accumulation of stocks; it is in these first three relations that the short-run production decisions first manifest themselves. Turning now to the medium and long run respectively, the next two equations explain the change in the labor force, both employed and unemployed, and the change in capital stock, or gross investment. Price of course maintains equilibrium in the production equations, but is determined explicitly, by producers, in the next equation. The rewards of factors are now explained: labor earnings are determined by a rate of change equation reflecting mainly bargaining strengths, and profits are given by the identity between income and product (or as an alternative, in terms of the overall prosperity of, and degree of competition in, the industry). Finally, two fixed proportions indicate the intermediate demand for the industry's product and the material prices facing the industry.

Conventions

Equations are discussed individually, and are identified by the name (which should not be interpreted as more than a label) and number (Roman for producers' equations, Greek for consumer's) given in the relevant heading. Variables and industries are represented by the symbols used in Chapter 3. Where necessary, variables carry an industry superscript (for example x^n), though in the interests of clarity this is often omitted when there is no possibility of confusion. Also for clarity, no time subscript is attached to current values of variables, and all nonsubscripted variables should be interpreted accordingly; the value of a variable τ periods before the present period is indicated by the addition of the subscript $-\tau$ (for example x^n_{-1}).

Unknown numerical parameters are represented by lowercase Greek letters with one superscript and two subscripts. In the industry models these are represented by α^i_{jk}, where i refers to the industry (though, as for variables, this identification is often omitted), j refers to the equation (of the outline model), and k refers to the particular term of this equation. For simplicity, the aggregate of the constant, seasonal terms (A, B, and C) and residual (ω^i_j) which appear in all stochastic equations is represented by γ^i_j, again with i referring to the industry and j to the equation. Thus a typical (the j-th) equation (say relating y to x) for industry i, which would in full be written as

$$y^i = \alpha^i_{j0} + \alpha^i_{j1} x^i + \alpha^i_{j2} A + \alpha^i_{j3} B + \alpha^i_{j4} C + \omega^i_j ,$$

would more simply be written as

$$y = \alpha_{j1} x + \gamma_j .$$

A similar notation is used in the final model. Here parameters are written as $\beta^{\mathbf{i}}_{jk}$, with **i** referring to the (industry identifying the) consumer category, j to the equation, and k to the variable. The composites of constant, seasonals, and residual are written as $\delta^{\mathbf{i}}_{j}$.

In the interests of consistency all industry models have the same number of equations, even though, as will be recalled from Chapter 3, some industry variables are available only in partially aggregated form—stocks for **evh** and **po**, and prices for **evho**. In these cases the stock for each industry of a group of size k is taken as $1/k$ times the total, and the price for the industry is taken as being the price for the total. This convention is adopted for simplicity. The alternative of using partially aggregated equations for these variables would be equivalent if all relations were linear; as they are not, small differences may arise. A similar point concerns the treatment of the price for industry **n**, which is not available; this is defined as being the price for **m**, the standard price equation for this industry being replaced by this identity.

4.2 PRODUCERS MODELS

It is now possible to specify the equations of the producers' or industry models: as has been noted, this is simply the specification of the standard outline model.

Demand (1)

This, though important, is not in itself a particularly interesting equation; if data were perfect it would be an identity: total demand for an industry's product is the sum of all individual demands. However, the composition of many components of demand in terms of their industry origin are not known, so this equation in effect estimates these proportions. Treating this as a production decision equation which seeks to explain the production decision in terms of lagged final demand, acting as a proxy for stocks, does not seem as satisfactory: there is nothing to be gained from postulating a rather tentative hypothesis concerning entrepreneurial behavior, when a logically safer approach would explain as much, albeit indirectly. This of course is only valid as stock formation is explained explicitly.

As the equation is of the nature of an accounting identity, variables are in money values. The most important components may be expected to be demands by other industries (g), followed by one or more types of final demand. This is an exception to the rule of generality in the outline model: one or more categories of final demand are selected to represent the demand structure facing each industry. Finally, total changes in stocks held by the industry are included, since these constitute the demand by the industry for its own product to hold as stocks. This does not allow for the changes of stocks of raw materials, and conversely for stocks of the industry's product held by other industries, for 'intermediate demand' measures only 'intermediate consumption.' It is outside the scope of this model to investigate the changes in composition of stocks, though stocks of the industry's product held by other industries might be reflected by the total (that is all industries') changes in stocks. Other factors however might well swamp the one to be identified in such a formulation, and this is not pursued.

The nature of this equation is perhaps unusual, and it should be emphasized that it is essentially an accounting relation rather than an explanation of economic behavior. Its stochastic form is due to the lack of data, and emphasizes the fact that estimates of data are just as stochastic as estimates of behavioral parameters. In practice, however, a line must be drawn somewhere, and this more rigorous treatment is only applied to 'fixed' proportions such as these parameters, which are not supplied as data in Chapter 3.

To summarize, equation 1 of the outline industry model takes the form

$$p^i x^i = \alpha^i_{11} p^i g^i + \alpha^i_{12} \varphi(i) + \alpha^i_{13} \psi(i) + \alpha^i_{14} (s^i - s^i_{-1}) + \gamma^i_1 \ ,$$

where $\varphi(i)$ and $\psi(i)$ are the final demand categories associated with industry i. These are given in Table 4-1, the rationale of which is self-explanatory. (The entry Σi in the table denotes aggregate investment; for notational simplicity all aggregates are written this way—so the symbol Σx is an abbreviation for $\sum_{i \in I} x^i$.)

Supply (2)

The (so called) supply function is a technological production function: output depends on inputs, all in physical units; it is central to the whole industry model.

Production is a field in which the usual practice of linearization may be inappropriate, for a linear function implies that the marginal products of each factor are independent of the amounts employed, and that the elasticity of substitution (between two factors) is infinite, giving perfect substitutability. An

Table 4-1. Final Demands

i	φ (i)	ψ (i)
n	n	m
f	c	–
c	F	–
s	m	J
e	Σi	m
v	c	n
h	J	–
t	m	–
p	c	n
o	n	–

alternative is the well-known logarithmic function (that is linear in logarithms), which implies declining marginal productivities of each factor and a finite elasticity of substitution—though this is always unity. Perhaps the most important generalization of this is the homohypallagic function, which allows the elasticity of substitution to assume any (positive) constant value. The linear function has the practical advantage of simplicity, and also the conceptual one of being meaningfully aggregable as it is additively separable; the other two functions do not share this important property. A linear function is therefore used; this may of course be considered as an approximation to some true function.

As this equation is of basic importance the logarithmic alternative was also estimated: the most relevant aspects of the adopted and alternative formulations, their implied marginal productivities, are given in the discussion of the estimates of the equation in Chapter 5.

The production function, then, is linear in inputs, and the question of how to define inputs arises. The prime input is labor, which may be defined in many ways; ideally, allowance should be made for hours worked (which can incorporate the distinction between part- and full-time labor), for quality, and for activity—particularly whether engaged in production or overhead work. Of these perhaps the most important is hours worked, and the exclusion of this variable can only be justified by the need for simplicity in the industry models. Hours and stocks are generally considered to be two of the most important peripheral (that is apart from the main output and income components) factors in short term models, and their usefulness in terms of explanatory power overlaps at least to some extent. Stocks are preferred for inclusion partly because they are a component of gross domestic product, albeit a small one, and partly because of some difficulty in identifying work input, or even hours worked, with hours registered. Quality and activity are perhaps less important, and more difficult to measure; both are omitted. The labor input, then, is simply the number of persons employed.

The second factor is capital, for which there are two important considerations: the use of gross or net stock, and allowance for utilization. Net stock, by allowing for depreciation, attempts to take into account the lower contribution made to output by older stock. Clearly older stock is less productive than (established) new stock (or at the most equally productive—otherwise it would be reproduced), but there are great difficulties in calculating this effect. A statistical approach runs into identification problems if the results are to be used in a production function, and the use of arbitrary or accounting measures is clearly open to error—the latter particularly by exaggerating depreciation (even to the point of 'writing off' stock still in use and thus giving it an infinite average product). The ideal approach of treating each vintage of capital as a separate input is not practical here. Accordingly, and as the original data is in gross terms, gross figures are used.

This gives a figure for capital capacity, and it now becomes desirable to allow for capital not in use—which clearly cannot contribute to current output. There are three main ways of achieving this: adjustment according to the unemployment of labor, adjustment according to the consumption of some material input directly connected with activity—for example electricity, and the explicit use of full capacity output. The first of these is used, mainly because this needs no data not already required by the model. This gives a measure

$$k_u = k_c \, l/(l+u) \, ,$$

where k_u and k_c are capital in use and capital stock respectively. This assumes that the proportional utilization of labor force and capital stock are equal. The use of electricity consumption is similar—it postulates a fixed ratio between capital input (or use) and another input; it is not used because of the unavailability of data and the need either to explain electricity consumption or (unsatisfactorily) to leave it exogenous. The essence of the full capacity method is the derivation of figures for full capacity output by plotting actual output, marking off cyclical peaks, and connecting these by straight lines; capacity utilization is then given by the ratio of the actual output to full capacity output. The objection to this approach is not that it relies on subjective definition of peaks but that it is only of use in the sample period, for the height and timing of the next peak must be known to predict current output. The capital input then is gross stock at the start of the period adjusted by the proportionate utilization of the labor force.

The conventional third factor of production is land; as usual this must be omitted due to lack of data. It is unlikely to be significant in a developed economy.

Allied to the main factors of production is their quality as embodied in technical change; a proper treatment of this subject is outside the scope of this study. A time trend, which might at least capture autonomous innovation, is not incorporated, because of the high expected collinearity between time and capital stock, even capital in use.

Finally, there is the question of nonfactor, or material, inputs. Ideally net output, or value added, should be used as the dependent variable, when material inputs would clearly be irrelevant. However, gross output is used, as a proxy for net output (as mentioned in Chapter 3), and the omission of material inputs is justified to the same extent that the use of this proxy is justified.

Thus equation 2 is (now dropping the industry superscript)

$$x = \alpha_{21} \, l + \alpha_{22} \, k_{-1} \, l/(l+u) + \gamma_2 \, .$$

Stocks (3)

As was indicated in the discussion of the exclusion of hours, the accumulation of inventories is one of the more important variables in the explanation of short-term fluctuations; it is also notoriously difficult to explain. Stock formation is treated as being basically voluntary (perhaps an undesirable assumption, but one which is usually necessary because of the difficulty of inferring the relative amounts that are voluntary and involuntary), and is explained by two factors: a modified accelerator effect and a speculative price effect.

The well-known simple accelerator approach depends on the hypothesis that a fixed amount of stocks must be held in order to produce smoothly a given output (here for simplicity in money values, which is equivalent to assuming that the price of stocks is proportional to the price of output), so that

$$s / px = \kappa$$

where $\kappa > 0$ is a constant. Taking first differences over τ period produces the familiar form

$$s - s_{-\tau} = \kappa (px - p_{-\tau} x_{-\tau}) \ .$$

Since stock adjustment is essentially a short-term phenomenon a lag of one quarter is used, so τ is unity. This simple form has various defects, perhaps the most important of which, particularly with quarterly data, is the omission of expectations, for it is clearly preferable to postulate that stock formation depends on the expected rather than the actual (and thus unobserved) change of output. Alternatively, making come concession to partially involuntary accumulation, intended rather than actual stock formation may depend on the change of output. Either of these important modifications may be expressed (as shown in Section 4.1) in the form

$$s - s_{-1} = \kappa (px - p_{-1} x_{-1}) + \pi (s_{-1} - s_{-2})$$

instead of the form above, where $\pi \in [0, 1]$ is another parameter; this modification is adopted.

Another motive for stockbuilding is speculative: stocks may be added to because of an expected price rise, either for raw materials or output. The rate of change of price (or output) over the last quarter is therefore included as being a rather naive indicator of the best estimate of the change in price over the current quarter.

The form of the equation for stocks is then

$$s - s_{-1} = \alpha_{31} (px - p_{-1} x_{-1}) + \alpha_{32} p/p_{-1} + \alpha_{33} (s_{-1} - s_{-2}) + \gamma_3 \ .$$

Labor (4)

This equation expresses the hypothesis that factor supply in an industry is determined by the relative remuneration of the factor in the industry; thus labor force is a function of relative earnings, and also of total labor availability. As this is a supply function, the relevant dependent variable is total labor offered, that is labor plus unemployment.

Earnings rather than wages are used because of the rather arbitrary definitions of basic wages. This is particularly relevant to an industry study as the difference between basic wage and average, or even 'standard,' earnings varies greatly from industry to industry. There are two relevant assumptions implicit in the use of earnings rather than wages: that there must be reasonable knowledge of earnings in different industries (or at least as good as that of wages), and that there should be no significant disutility of work in the relevant range—or an industry will not attract labor by offering high wages if this calls for a proportionately greater increase in work. This applies particularly as weekly rather than hourly earnings are used, for then the total amount of work as well as its possible unpleasantness is relevant. Though clearly not ideally satisfied, these assumptions may well be acceptable in practice, or at least preferable to those implied by the use of wages.

The general availability of labor is of direct importance. This is included as an explanatory variable, rather than simply dividing the dependent variable by it, because of the desirability of partitioning the total labor force into those employed and those not employed—presumably the latter would be more mobile. It is relevant to mention here the rather arbitrary nature of figures for unemployment by industry, for these refer to those who were last employed in the industry, not necessarily those who are seeking employment in the industry. It may be possible to allow for this by a complex lag structure for unemployment, based on figures of the average duration of unemployment, but this is not attempted.

The labor equation is therefore of the form

$$l + u = \alpha_{41} e \, \Sigma \, l / \Sigma el + \alpha_{42} \Sigma l + \alpha_{43} \Sigma u + \gamma_4$$

(Note that $\Sigma l / \Sigma el$ is simply the inverse of average earnings, so that the first term reflects relative earnings, as required.)

Investment (5)

Capital formation has long been recognized as being of prime importance in explaining medium-term fluctuations and long-term growth. There are two main hypotheses concerning the determinants of this, in the form of net investment demand: the accelerator approach and the profits hypothesis. These, in modified forms, are combined in the capital equation.

The simple accelerator hypothesis is equivalent to that discussed above for inventory investment; it presupposes a fixed capital-output ratio, and is thus theoretically inappropriate when confronted with the typical excess capacity of cyclical decline, though may be a useful approximation and thus frequently acceptable in practice. The essence of investment is expectation, since investment necessarily involves the future; the accelerator is therefore modified by a distributed lag expectations hypothesis, or alternatively this may be interpreted as an imperfect adjustment process to some desired level of capital stock (though this is more properly allowed for in the discussion of depreciation). As with inventory investment, the value of sales is used, but here more permanent changes are relevant, reflected by the change over the last year, that is four periods.

The profits hypothesis may either be interpreted as past profits being an indicator of future profits and thus of the marginal efficiency of capital, or as profits being a proxy for liquidity (either through being retained or through influencing possible lenders) on which investment depends. The choice of the specific form of the profits variable to be included is somewhat arbitrary; the last year's post-tax profit is adopted. The deduction of tax is relevant whichever interpretation of the profits hypothesis is preferred; indeed, if the scope of the model allowed it might be preferable to deduct dividends as well, leaving solely additions to reserves.

These two factors are relevant to the determination of net investment, and as the dependent variable is gross investment, an allowance must be made for replacement investment, approximated by depreciation. This is assumed to be proportional to capital stock and so capital at the start of the quarter is included as an explanatory variable. An equally important reason for including the stock at the start of the quarter concerns a desired stock, or imperfect adjustment process, hypothesis: that there is a desired stock of capital which depends on the above factors, but only some fraction of the difference between this and the actual stock is made up in each quarter. If this fraction is represented by a constant $\kappa \in [0, 1]$, and the desired and actual stocks by k_d and k respectively, then net investment i_n is given by

$$i_n = \kappa(k_d - k_{-1}),$$

and so capital at the start of the period has an inhibiting effect on net investment. This effect then works in opposition to the depreciation effect.

Equation 5 thus takes the form

$$i = \alpha_{51}(px - p_{-4}x_{-4}) + \alpha_{52} \sum_{\tau=1}^{4} z_{-\tau}(1 - R_{-\tau}) + \alpha_{53}k_{-1} + \alpha_{54}i_{-1} + \gamma_5.$$

(Note that the second term simply reflects last year's post-tax profits).

Price (6)

The price formation equation is a markup relation modified by supply and demand considerations, the dependent variable being the wholesale output price.

The first element of cost is that of raw materials purchased (h). This is straightforward.

The next element is that of labor; this is taken as unit labor costs, that is the ratio of total labor payments to output. No attempt is made to investigate the hypothesis that permanent rather than transitory changes determine markups, and that changes in basic wage rates are considered as permanent whereas changes in the difference between earnings and wages are transitory. This is one of the prices that must be paid for omitting basic wages from the model.

This theory of price formation is essentially short run: past expenditure on capital is irrelevant. For this reason no account is taken of 'capital costs,' or even of depreciation.

The forces of demand and supply are taken into account, though they do not appear explicitly; the excess of supply over demand is represented by the ratio of stocks to output at the start of the quarter. Again, no account is taken of permanent and transitory factors—for example by using deviation from a trend. An alternative measure of the relative strengths of supply and demand might be inferred from capacity utilization, but the low degree of confidence in the proxy for this adopted here prohibits its use other than for its basic purpose, that of adjusting capital stock.

Since the dependent variable is wholesale price no account need be taken of consumer taxes, since these are not levied directly on the producer (though excise duties are levied on the producer and should enter into the wholesale price, but the model does not incorporate these).

The adopted form of the price equation is then

$$p = \alpha_{61} h + \alpha_{62} el/x + \alpha_{63} s_{-1} x_{-1} + \gamma_6 .$$

Earnings (7)

The earnings equation is a condensation of what should ideally be a whole sector, explaining standard hours, basic wage rate, overtime rate, and bonuses, and connected by the relevant identities. If the omission of hours is accepted then the arbitrary nature of the relation between wages and earnings across industries justifies to some extent this condensation. Besides simplicity, this has the advantage of representing a more continuous phenomenon, for typically wage bargaining is an annual process while the more fundamental variable, earnings, fluctuates more according to the factors affecting it. Salary rates are more open to individual bargaining and more responsive to economic factors than wage rates, and it is interesting in this context to note the close correlation between salary earnings and wage earnings (but not wage rates) mentioned in Chapter 3. As is usual, rates of change are relevant, and so the rate of change of earnings is expressed as a function of four factors: unemployment, and the rates of change of output, of profits, and of consumer prices.

Unemployment is of course the basic explanatory variable for the wage element in earnings. Industry rather than total unemployment is used: if there were perfect mobility between industries this would not be relevant, but it seems clear that mobility is far from perfect in the short run. It may be expected that the effect of a change in unemployment would be greater when unemployment is low than when it is high, partly because of underemployment when unemployment is high and partly because money wages very seldom fall whatever the state of unemployment; that is, the rate of change of (money) wages has a floor at zero and so the rate of change of earnings may be expected to have a 'soft floor' somewhere below zero. For this reason the level of unemployment is replaced by (minus) its reciprocal. It is relevant to note that unemployment does not perfectly reflect the more fundamental factor relevant here, the excess of supply over demand in the labor market. Ideally, unfilled vacancies should be taken into account, but this is not attempted.

Just as unemployment may be relevant in explaining the wage element in total earnings, output may be relevant in explaining the hours element. This reflects the practice of using existing resources more fully during a period of temporary pressure on demand (or during the early stages of a more permanent increase in demand), rather than increasing actual resources. The essence of this is that it is a short run phenomenon; in the medium run more labor is hired, in the long run more capital is used. To incorporate this effect the rate of change of output over the last quarter is included.

Profits are included for two reasons. Firstly, they may be relevant in the bargaining process even if they are not known by labor, for the existence of high profits shifts the contract curve to labor's advantage by increasing the opportunity cost to capital of a strike; further, as negotiation becomes more centralized and frequently carried out under public and governmental surveillance, high profits tend to sway public opinion and government intervention to the side of labor. Secondly, it may frequently benefit the capitalist to maintain a generous remuneration structure where this can be afforded in order to attract high efficiency labor, or at least maintain a satisfied (and therefore quiet) labor force; this is particularly relevant where it is realized that abnormally high profit margins in oligopoly will attract new entrants, or possibly the attention of antitrust bodies. Profits then are included, in the form of the proportional increase over the last year—since quarterly changes are probably not known, or discounted, by the capitalist.

Finally, the inclusion of the change in consumer prices reflects the absence of (complete) money illusion in the labor market, where an increase in consumer prices may both raise the supply price of labor and swing public and official opinion to its side. This gives the earnings equation in the form

$$e/e_{-1} = \alpha_{71}/u + \alpha_{72} x/x_{-1} + \alpha_{73} z/z_{-4} + \alpha_{74} \Sigma bc \Sigma c_{-4}/\Sigma b_{-4} c_{-4} \Sigma c + \gamma_7 .$$

(In the fourth term Σc is of course aggregate consumption $\sum_{i \in I} c^i$, though as there are only four categories of consumption ($i \in C$), it is equivalently $\sum_{i \in I} c^i$. Thus the whole fourth term simply reflects the overall change in consumer prices over the last year.)

Profits (8)

Profits are simply the difference between the value added, or value of net product, and the wage bill. To obtain the former the index of value added must be multiplied by the base μ referred to in Chapter 3; the latter is straightforward.

This gives

$$z = \mu p x - e l \ .$$

(Note that this is a deterministic not stochastic relationship, so there are no α to be estimated, nor γ.)

Alternative Profits

It was mentioned above that, because of the importance of profits, an alternative formulation would be considered. In fact, purely theoretical arguments suggest that the basic formulation is the more appropriate; the alternative is really considered to see whether the theoretically better form is empirically better. This alternative is a 'quasibehavioral' relation, based on Evans' model of profits.

The main determinant of profits is sales, for this provides the dividend to be shared between the factors of production, and where factor shares are relatively stable the total dividend of each industry may be expected to be the prime determinant of the share of each factor in the industry.

In an indirect examination of the determinants of profits Kuh [p. 234] proposes that 'the basic determinants of cyclical variations in corporate profits arise from cyclical variations in labor productivity.' Labor productivity is included here indirectly through unit labor costs, since as Evans [p. 348] points out, 'it is more reasonable to relate profits to changes in unit labor costs than to changes in productivity.' Evans' formulation however takes no explicit account of labor productivity or unit labor costs. Instead, a measure of capacity utilization is included which acts as a proxy for the relevant part of labor productivity, or the part of labor costs that does not vary with output. This is mainly the cost of overhead workers who must be employed even when output is low (and also usually employed at a fixed level of remuneration), but also applies to production workers through labor hoarding due to the costs of hiring and dismissal. As no very reliable measure of capacity utilization is contained in this model, unit labor costs are included explicitly. It should be stressed that unit labor costs are not included as costs per se, but as a proxy for some part of productivity; thus an increase in unit labor costs need not be associated with a fall in profits—an increase of unit labor costs under conditions of full markup and low elasticity of demand will increase profits.

One reason why past sales may be expected to be relevant is that this term might reflect the (positive or negative) effect of lagged wage responses. This becomes redundant because of the explicit inclusion of unit labor costs, though there are two more important reasons for its inclusion; firstly, that it may reflect increases in fixed costs resulting from capital expenditure stimulated by prior increases in sales, and secondly, that it may allow for more firms being induced to enter the industry and result in an increase in competition and loss of economies of scale. It is the second of these which is taken as being the more relevant here; the first could be included explicitly if required. The lag used should reflect the time taken by outsiders to enter the industry; this is taken to be a year.

The interpretation of profits makes any consideration of payments for interest or royalties irrelevant, for they are all part of the reward of fixed factors. Inventory valuation adjustments may however be relevant, for profits are ostensibly measured before providing for stock appreciation, that is including any capital gains or losses from holding inventories. As this formulation of the profits relationship is relevant to the profit derived from production rather than speculation, an allowance for the change in value of existing inventories, though not of course the value of the physical increase, should be appropriate. However, there is good reason to believe that although reported profits should take changes in the value of existing inventories into account they probably do not, especially if values rise, mainly because of the conservative and arbitrary nature of corporate accounting. It is thus assumed, here and throughout, that the changes in values of inventories are not included in the profit figures used, and so all income terms are interpreted as being income from production alone, which is what is desired. This assumption may not be ideally satisfied, but seems preferable to the only viable alternative—that full account is taken of increases in the value of existing inventories.

It should be noted that this stochastic equation need not prove more accurate than the deterministic one in the context of the whole model for two reasons. Firstly, data inaccuracies, or the fact that the bases μ are strictly estimates, mean that the equation itself need not hold identically in prediction. Secondly, small errors in the predicted values of the two quantities between which profits is the difference, will entail a large error in the predicted value of profits, whereas the quasibehavioral formulation does not express profits as a residual difference between two similar series, and also is 'anchored' to some extent by the predetermined lagged sales term.

The alternative profits equation therefore takes the form

$$z = \alpha_{81}\, px + \alpha_{82}\, el/x + \alpha_{83}\, p_{-4}\, x_{-4} + \gamma_8 \ .$$

Intermediate Demand (9)

The intermediate demand for an industry's product is the sum of all industries' demands (including its own—because of the conventions of the input-output accounting system used). Now the demand by industry j for the product of industry i is simply the input-output coefficient λ^{ij} (that is the demand for output of i by j per unit output of j) multiplied by the output of j—adjusted by its weight v^j.

This (deterministic) equation is therefore

$$g^i = \sum_{j \in I} \lambda^{ij} v^j x^j \,.$$

Materials Price (10)

The overall price of materials purchased by an industry is a weighted sum of the (output) prices of all industries (including itself) which supply these materials. The weights are simply the relative importance of these suppliers, that is, for industry **i**, the input-output coefficient λ^{ji}. As a convention this weighted sum is normalized to make it a weighted average.

It should be noted that this formulation omits any reference to imported materials. This is unfortunate, but the scope of the model does not allow it.

The final equation of the outline industry model is then

$$h^i = \sum_{j \in I} \lambda^{ji} p^j \Big/ \sum_{j \in I} \lambda^{ji} \,.$$

4.3 CONSUMERS MODEL

There is only one consumer's model. This covers all final demand: that relating to consumers proper, to government, and to the rest of the world. However, since government activity is treated exogenously, the explanation covers only two areas: consumption and trade. It is recalled that the former is divided into four categories (these associated with the outputs of industries **f**, **v**, **t**, and **o**), and the second into two categories (**m** and **n**). These relations are now discussed.

Consumption (i)

Consumption functions are of the Keynesian form, with allowances for expectations and relative prices.

It is natural to use disposable rather than pretax income to reflect purchasing power, but there remain problems whether to include profits and transfer payments. If the model explained the distribution of profits then one would simply include dividends; however, this is not the case, and since much profit is not distributed, and also since capitalists are generally supposed to have lower propensities to consume than workers, profits are not included in the income term. Transfer payments are all distributed, and typically to those with high consumption propensities; naturally these are included. The income term is then disposable labor income, that is total (industry plus government) earnings plus transfer payments, all after tax.

In practice, it is expected rather than actual income which primarily determines consumption. A simple distributed lag form is adopted to capture this effect. The lag is one quarter; this simple form seems preferable to using the last four (say) quarters' consumption, which would embody the alternative hypothesis of the existence of some normal level of consumption from which adjustments to current conditions are made. No attempt is made to separate the transitory and permanent components of income, or to use other time-oriented effects, such as the life-cycle or ratchet hypotheses.

Income, or expected income, will only determine aggregate consumption; its division among categories will depend on relative prices. These are represented by the ratio of the price for the category to the general consumer price level—the weighted (by consumption) average of the prices for all categories. Effects depending on absolute prices, such as speculation, are ignored.

The consumption equations therefore take the form

$$c = \beta_{11} (\Sigma el + W + V)(1 - T) + \beta_{12} b \Sigma c / \Sigma bc + \beta_{13} c_{-1} + \delta_1 .$$

Consumer Price (ii)

Ideally, the determination of consumer prices should be an activity of the retailing industry, but the necessary aggregation within nonmanufacturing makes it more appropriate to treat this here.

Consumer prices are determined by a simple markup process from the corresponding wholesale (or output) prices, with an allowance now for the effect of purchase taxes.

The consumer price equations are

$$b = \beta_{21} p + \beta_{22} D + \delta_2 .$$

Imports (iii)

Since the main purpose of the model is to illuminate interaction within the economy, external links (imports and exports) are treated very simply.

Import demand for each of the two trade categories is determined by expected domestic income. The income term is total labor income (earnings, profits, and government); expectations are incorporated through a distributed lag term.

This gives the form

$$m = \beta_{31} (\Sigma el + \Sigma z + W) + \beta_{32} m_{-1} + \delta_3 .$$

Exports (iv)

Export demand is treated analogously to import demand, only aggregate purchasing power is represented by the volume of world trade rather than domestic income. The use of volume rather than value of world trade is an exception to the use of values for behavioral relations; despite the inconsistency this seems preferable where the relevant price is an external price affected by inflation and currency revaluation throughout the world.

This gives the equation

$$n = \beta_{41} Q + \beta_{42} n_{-1} + \delta_4 .$$

4.4 MODEL AS A WHOLE

Having specified the whole model by specifying the individual agent's models, it is constructive to see how these fit together.

Interaction

It is clear that the individual agent's models are highly interdependent. These interdependencies, or linkages, may conveniently be partitioned into two types: horizontal linkages, which are direct linkages between agents, and vertical linkages, which are indirect, acting through aggregates.

Another way of looking at these is in terms of Klein's two categories of multisectoral econometric model. The first of these is the 'general to particular' model, where an agent's model is grafted into an existing aggregate model, while the second is essentially the Leontief input-output model. The model presented here combines both these approaches through its vertical and horizontal linkages respectively.

The formal specification of the model avoids, or solves for, any purely definitional variables and relations (for example wage bill equals earnings multiplied by labor); in other words all relations involve nontrivial (known or unknown) parameters. This makes their number have some relevance. There are ten endogenous variables and equations associated with each of the ten industry models, and twelve of each with the consumer's model, making a total of 112. However, as mentioned in Section 4.1, the price relation for industry n (or m) and the stocks relations for industries v and h (or e and h, or h and v) and for industry p (or o) are not independent; this reduces the number of independent relations and endogenous variables to 109. There are also twelve purely exogenous variables (exclusively government and external variables), and various lagged endogenous variables—including capital, which is always lagged, and so not counted in the 109 figure. In the theoretical framework of Chapter 2, the model is therefore a mapping from the 109-dimensional euclidean space into itself.

Total Product

The model has not (explicitly) used the concept of total product, that is total income or expenditure, and more importantly, has not ensured the conceptual identity between these. The reason for this is of course that *measured* income and expenditure are not in general equal, but differ by some residual error.

There are two ways of treating this discrepancy: one may define the measured quantities in such a way as to make them equal, and in effect take the error out of a component of one of them—typically the residual, profits, or alternatively one may accept the discrepancy in the data (and see whether the model preserves this within tolerable limits). Since an error is in practice unavoidable it is preferable to include this explicitly, and so use data series which are individually considered to be most accurate, rather than introducing the error implicitly, and thus distorting the measurement of one or more variables. Since industry behavior is motivated by profits, and profits, being defined as a residual, are usually made to absorb the full discrepancy when this is to be 'hidden,' this is particularly relevant here.

If these concepts are required, total income is simply the sum of all factor incomes, so one may define this as

$$y^* = \Sigma el + \Sigma z + W.$$

Similarly, total expenditure is the sum of the (net) expenditures on all the components of final demand, with the usual allowance for indirect taxes to reduce this from market price to the more meaningful factor cost basis (which makes it comparable with total income). One may then define total expenditure as

$$y0 = \Sigma c(1 - D) + \Sigma i + \Sigma (s - s_{-1}) + F + W + J + N - M.$$

Summary

For convenient reference, the formal relations of the model are collected together here. Equations (1)–(10) apply for each $i \in I$, equations (i) and (ii) for each $i \in C$, and equations (iii) and (iv) for $i \in \{m, n\}$ (whether or not the index i is explicit). Variables and parameters are given in Appendix A, and the functions φ and ψ in Table 4-1; variables represented by capital letters are exogenous.

1. $p^i x^i = \alpha^i_{11} p^i g^i + \alpha^i_{12} \varphi(i) + \alpha^i_{13} \psi(i) + \alpha^i_{14} (s^i - s^i_{-1}) + \gamma^i_1$

2. $x = \alpha_{21} l + \alpha_{22} k_{-1} l/(l + u) + \gamma_2$

3. $s - s_{-1} = \alpha_{31} (px - p_{-1} x_{-1}) + \alpha_{32} p/p_{-1} + \alpha_{33} (s_{-1} - s_{-2}) + \gamma_3$

4. $l + u = \alpha_{41} e \Sigma l/\Sigma el + \alpha_{42} \Sigma l + \alpha_{43} \Sigma u + \gamma_4$

5. $i = \alpha_{51} (px - p_{-4} x_{-4}) + \alpha_{52} \sum_{\tau=1}^{4} z_{-\tau}(1 - R_{-\tau}) + \alpha_{53} k_{-1} + \alpha_{54} i_{-1} + \gamma_5$

6. $p = \alpha_{61} h + \alpha_{62} el/x + \alpha_{63} s_{-1}/x_{-1} + \gamma_6$

7. $e/e_{-1} = \alpha_{71}/u + \alpha_{72} x/x_{-1} + \alpha_{73} z/z_{-4} + \alpha_{74} \Sigma bc \Sigma c_{-4}/\Sigma b_{-4} c_{-4} \Sigma c + \gamma_7$

8. $z = \mu px - el$

9. $g^i = \sum_{j \in I} \lambda^{ij} \mu^j x^j$

10. $h^i = \sum_{j \in I} \lambda^{ji} p^j / \sum_{j \in I} \lambda^{ji}$

(i) $c = \beta_{11} (\Sigma el + W + V)(1 - T) + \beta_{12} b \, \Sigma c / \Sigma bc + \beta_{13} c_{-1} + \delta_1$

(ii) $b = \beta_{21} p + \beta_{22} D + \delta_2$ 3

(iii) $m = \beta_{31} (\Sigma el + \Sigma z + W) + \beta_{32} m_{-1} + \delta_3$

(iv) $n = \beta_{41} Q + \beta_{42} n_{-1} + \delta_4$

Chapter Five

Estimated Model

Action rules are now specified, up to a number of unknown real-valued parameters, for each of the agents; also, a body of observed data on the behavior of these agents is available. One must now relate this data to the theory, or in other words, estimate, by some appropriate method of statistical inference, the values of the parameters, and thus complete the specification of the agents' action rules.

This is considered in the present chapter. There is however a complication: when confronted with, or in effect tested by, the data, various aspects of the theoretical model might prove inappropriate, and might therefore need modification; this is also considered. Again, the producing agents and the consuming agent are discussed separately. However, before one may do this it is appropriate to consider the question of statistical inference, or the theory of estimation; the chapter commences with such a discussion.

5.1 ESTIMATION THEORY

The problem is the following: given a model M involving a vector α of unknown parameters, and an array of data X, what is an appropriate estimation rule φ, giving

$$\alpha = \varphi(M, X) \ ?$$

It is a problem of basic importance, for the estimated model, that is (M, α), the tool of the quantitative analysis, depends on φ. (Here, and throughout this section, the notation is an abstract one, not related to that of Chapters 3 and 4).

Maximum Likelihood
The fundamental meaning of 'estimation' is the determination of the 'most likely' values of the true parameters of the model; true parameters are

population parameters, which are essentially unknown (at least in a time series model where the population is not finite). Alternatively, one may interpret estimation as the determination of the values of the parameters which are most likely to generate the observed sample of data; this interpretation, the maximum likelihood method is adopted.

More formally, let $f(x; \alpha)$ be the frequency function of the random variable x when α is the value of the parameter vector to be estimated; if $x_1, \ldots x_n$ are the values of x corresponding to each of the T (independent) observations on this variable, then the joint probability of observing these values (in order) when the parameter is α, $L(x_1, \ldots x_T; \alpha)$, is the product of the individual probabilities, so

$$L(x_1, \ldots x_T; \alpha) = f(x_1; \alpha) \ldots f(x_T; \alpha) \quad ;$$

the function L is the likelihood function. The maximum likelihood method then takes $(x_1, \ldots x_n)$ as fixed and finds the value of α which maximizes this function, now written $L(\alpha)$. As is well known, this is equivalent to the familiar least squares method, which in effect chooses the value of α that minimizes the sum of squares of the errors of the 'predictions' of x.

The simple maximum likelihood method concerns the conditional distribution of just one variable, given the values of a set of other (predetermined) variables. It is not however appropriate where there is more than one jointly dependent variable, for in such cases it is the joint conditional distribution given the values of other (predetermined) variables that is relevant. The model developed here is of this simultaneous form.

Schematically, one may represent this as follows. Let x_t be a vector of the h observed predetermined variables, y_t a vector of the g observed endogenous variables, and ω_t a vector of g residuals (one for each equation—or endogenous variable), all in period t, where $1 \leqslant t \leqslant T$. The linear model is then

$$By_t + \Gamma x_t = \omega_t \quad ,$$

where $B \equiv [\beta_{ij}]$ is a $g \times g$ matrix of the coefficients of the endogenous variables, and $\Gamma \equiv [\gamma_{ij}]$ a $g \times h$ matrix of those of the predetremined variables. The model may also be represented by its reduced form, which expresses the endogenous variables explicitly in terms of the predetermined variables and residuals. This may be written as

$$y_t = Px_t + v_t$$

where $P \equiv -B^{-1}\Gamma$ is the matrix of reduced form coefficients and $v_t \equiv B^{-1}\omega_t$ the vector of reduced form disturbances.

The relevant joint conditional distribution may be obtained by re-writing the reduced form equations as explicit functions for all the v_t, obtaining the joint normal distribution of these, and substituting for each in this its value from the reduced form, giving a joint conditional distribution of the y_t given the x_t and reduced form parameters. The reduced form parameters are then expressed in terms of the structural equation parameters, and this becomes the likelihood function of the (structural equation) parameters given the observed values of the y_t and x_t.

The maximum likelihood process then finds the B and Γ that maximizes the value of this likelihood function subject to all the a priori restrictions. This is a cumbersome process in practice (unless all the equations are just identified—when it is unnecessary) and so a compromise is frequently made, whereby only a part of the a priori restrictions is taken into account. At the limit there is the case where no a priori restrictions are taken into account; this is equivalent to estimating each equation in isolation, and is thus the method of ordinary least squares.

Thus there are two extreme methods for estimating the parameters of a system of equations: (full information) maximum likelihood (FIML) and (no information) ordinary least squares (OLS); there are also a number of so called limited information maximum likelihood methods between these two extremes. However, before examining these it is appropriate to discuss the concept of identification.

Identification

Identification may be defined as the process of determining the parameters of the structure from those of the likelihood function. It is logically prior to the estimation process itself, and may pose complex problems; it is only briefly discussed here since, as will become apparent, this model is substantially overidentified. The identification problem arises because one is concerned with relations between jointly endogenous variables; the fact that these variables are jointly endogenous implies that they are related in more ways than one. Thus the problem is how to be sure that one is estimating the parameters of the structural equation one intends, rather than some other relation between the endogenous variables; that is, how to identify which relation one is estimating. Any model may be written in its reduced form, and the parameters of this may be estimated without identification difficulty since there is only one relation—if there were not, the 'predetermined' variables would not be truly predetermined. However, the reduced form may not always be transformed back into the structural equations, and thus, as an identification problem can be encountered with the latter but not the former; one may interpret the identification problem as that of deducing the values of the structural parameters from the reduced form parameters. The reason why this interpretation is equivalent to the definition above is that the likelihood function may be written in terms of any observationally equivalent structure, for example the reduced form, that is

$$f(y_1, \ldots y_T; x_1, \ldots x_T) = f(v_1) \ldots f(v_T) \ .$$

Now since

$$v_t = y_t - Px_t$$

the parameters of the likelihood function become the matrix of reduced form coefficients P and the reduced form variance-covariance matrix. The latter is

$$V = E\, v_t\, v'_t = B^{-1}\, U B'^{-1}$$

where $U = E\, \omega_t\, \omega'_t$ is the structural form variance-covariance matrix (E is the expectations operation and a prime denotes transposition).

Thus the identification problem becomes one of making sure that P (or V) is such that the reduced form produces only one structural equation (or strictly one linear combination) complying with the restrictions placed on the relevant equation; thus identification may be achieved by imposing restrictions on P (or V). In practice, the most important restrictions are those on P, and of these the simplest are those of a zero-nonzero nature, that is specifying that certain elements in B and Γ are zero, or equivalently that certain variables appear only in certain equations. If this type of restriction is applied, a necessary condition for identification of an equation is that the number of variables excluded from it is at least equal to the number of equations less one. Expressing the number of endogenous and predetermined variables appearing in the relevant equation as g^* and h^* respectively, this condition is

$$j \equiv g - g^* + h - h^* \geqslant g - 1 \ ,$$

or

$$h - h^* \geqslant g^* - 1 \ ,$$

that is the number of predetermined variables excluded from the relation must not be less than the number of endogenous variables included less one. If $j < g - 1$ the equation is underidentified, if $j = g - 1$ the equation is just identified, and if $j > g - 1$ then it is overidentified. This order condition is not a sufficient condition for identification; there is also a necessary and sufficient rank condition, but this uses determinants involving the true values of the structural parameters, which are of course unknown. In practice, the necessary condition is usually deemed to be sufficient, for it is unlikely that the order condition would be satisfied without the rank condition also being satisfied; if the structural parameters are considered continuous then there is zero probability that the determinants which would need to be zero for this to happen would be zero—though they may be near zero, in which case the structural coefficients are ill-determined.

This discussion concerns the identification of a linear model, and is not directly applicable to a nonlinear model. However, if the model contains at least one true exogenous variable (that is excluding the constant term) then the conditions mentioned above apply; further, by in effect forming new exogenous variables, nonlinearities may aid identification.

It is apparent from the order condition that all the equations in this model are substantially overidentified, mainly because of lagged variables and nonlinearities. Ideally, one should attempt to test these hypothesized conditions for identifiability, since the a priori exclusion of variables is itself subject to uncertainty. This is not usually attempted in practice; it is omitted here because of the particularly strong prima facie case for overidentification.

Limited Information
Having briefly discussed identification one may now turn to the estimation methods in the range between FIML and OLS, known collectively as limited information methods. There is a wide range of such methods; the discussion is restricted to two of the most important—limited information maximum likelihood (LIML) and two stage least squares (TSLS).

The LIML method is so called because it finds values of the parameters that maximize the value of the likelihood function subject only to the a priori restrictions imposed on the equation being estimated. This constrained maximization is equivalent to minimizing the ratio, k, of the unexplained variance of y^* in its regression on all the predetermined variables included in the equation being estimated, to the unexplained variance of y^* in its regression on all the predetermined variables in the model, where y^* is a synthetic variable combining the g^* endogenous variables appearing in this (the i-th) equation.

$$y_t^* = \beta_{i1} y_{1t} + \ldots \beta_{ig*} y_{g*t'} \qquad (t = 1, \ldots T) \ .$$

The ratio k cannot be less than unity, for adding explanatory variables cannot increase the residual variance; at the extreme the added variables may have no effect, and $k = 1$. This is an explanation of the rationale of the method, for in seeking to minimize k it seeks to bring it as near to unity as possible, that is to find a parameter vector such that the predetermined variables omitted from the equation should make a minimal improvement in the fit y^*. The method is thus equivalent to the least variance ratio principle, which seeks to minimize k directly. It is central to the 'limited information' methods, for it may be shown that TSLS is a special case of FIML where k is set to unity, and also that OLS is a special case with k set to zero (this is not consistent with the definition of k, but then OLS is not a consistent method); these are some of the members of the family of k-class estimators developed by Theil.

Though the TSLS method may be thought of as a special case of LIML, its rationale is that the inconsistency of OLS estimation arises through the correlation between the disturbance term and the endogenous variables, so consistent estimators may be obtained by removing the stochastic component associated with the disturbance from the endogenous variables. To achieve this, one of the endogenous variables is selected as the dependent variable for each equation separately, and all the remaining endogenous variables in the equation are replaced by their estimated values in terms of all the predetermined variables, calculated from the least squares estimates of the reduced forms; the method of OLS is then applied to the modified structural equation. Clearly there is a basic similarity between TSLS and LIML, for both use all the predetermined variables in the model but do not require knowledge of the specifications of any equations other than the one being estimated; that is they utilize only the a priori information on that equation.

Assessment

The evaluation of the various estimation methods available is in two stages. At first it is assumed that the usual estimation requirements are satisfied: more specifically that there is no serious multicollinearity, serial correlation of disturbances, correlation between disturbances in different equations, or heteroskedasticity, and that there are no specification errors. At this level asymptotic properties are considered first, not because an infinite sample is envisaged, but because they are relatively tractable mathematically and may be useful approximations to small (or finite) sample properties. The asymptotic properties taken account of are consistency, normality, and efficiency. An estimator $\hat{\beta}$ of a parameter whose true value is β is asymptotically consistent if for all $\hat{\beta}$ the probability limit of $\hat{\beta}$ is β; this is not equivalent to asymptotic unbiasedness, which requires that $E\hat{\beta} = \beta$ in the limit, for the mean of the limiting distribution may not exist, in which case unbiasedness is not defined. The estimator is asymptotically normal if the limiting distribution $f_T(\beta)$, as T tends to infinity, is normal. The estimator is asymptotically efficient if it is consistent and normal and the variance of its limiting distribution is not greater than that of any other consistent and normal estimator. It may be shown that OLS is inconsistent (thus its efficiency is not defined, though by definition it has least variance) and TSLS, LIML, and FIML are all consistent, normal, and efficient (defined for the first two relative to other estimators using the same incomplete a priori information). Thus, apart from a possible reservation about OLS, asymptotic properties are of little help in the choice of a method for estimating this model.

Even if an examination of asymptotic properties were to give a clear ranking of estimation methods, this would not necessarily reflect the ranking of finite sample properties; further, asymptotic properties are frequently not defined, for they depend on the limiting distribution having finite first and second moments, and many estimators involve division by random variables that have nonzero probability densities at value zero. Small sample properties tend to be mathematically intractable and thus are often investigated experimentally, though some theoretical results have been obtained, but not enough to be decisive. There are also a number of empirical studies which may help in the evaluation of different methods, though these too are inevitably particular. These 'Monte Carlo' studies are simulation studies: a model is postulated with known parameters (including a known distribution function of the residuals), and a set of data is generated to be consistent with these parameters (and distribution of the residuals), then the required parameters are estimated by the methods being investigated. The estimation process is repeated a large number of times using different subsets of the data, thus generating probability distributions of estimates of the parameters under different estimation procedures. There are three conventional measures for interpreting the results of such experiments: bias, $E\hat{\beta} - \beta$; variance, $E(\hat{\beta} - E\hat{\beta})^2$; and mean-square-error, $E(\hat{\beta} - \beta)^2$. The first is bias in the usual sense, the second is the variance of the estimates around their mean, and the third is the variance of the estimates around the true value—which is equivalent to variance (around the mean) plus the square of the bias.

There are a number of such studies, which all tend to show that if the ideal estimation assumptions are fulfilled then FIML is the best estimator (in the three series considered), followed by LIML and TSLS together, and finally OLS, but if the ideal assumptions are relaxed them FIML becomes much inferior. The real problem is to differentiate between LIML and TSLS. A key to this is provided by Quandt, who examines two 4-equation models with a sample size of 20 and varying degrees of multicollinearity between the predetermined variables. It is found that TSLS is preferable to OLS until the degree of multicollinearity becomes very high, when OLS is preferred. Quandt also computes estimates for a series of 25 k-class estimators with k ranging from –0.4 to 2.0, and obtains the important result that the estimator is relatively insensitive to the value of k (the mean estimate over 100 samples is fairly constant) for values from –0.4 to around 1.0 and from around 1.3 to 2.0, but in the range in the middle the mean estimate fluctuates violently. This conclusion, that the LIML estimator may be highly unstable if k is in the region of 1.1 to 1.2, is reinforced by Theil, who estimates parameters by k-class methods for various values of k from real data (this is not a Monte Carlo experiment), and notices the same phenomenon.

In practice, the properties of estimators must be considered in conjunction with their robustness, both as regards mis-specification and as regards the failure to (approximately) satisfy the assumptions on which the theoretical properties are based: particularly the absence of multicollinearity and serial correlation. It is clear that FIML seriously lacks robustness: as the estimation of any equation depends on the specification of the entire model, any error in specification will tend to affect the estimates of all the parameters in the model. This is of particular importance in this model, where certain equations are of relatively unproven validity. At the practical level the complexity of FIML makes computation difficult, though not impossible for small systems (especially if more simple asymptotically equivalent forms are considered).

The fundamental difference between the two limited information methods being considered is that though both are members of the k-class of estimators, the value of k in LIML is stochastic, being the root of a stochastic determinental equation, whereas the value of k in TSLS is deterministic, being in effect defined as unity; this is why LIML may be expected to be the less robust. It may be recalled that TSLS requires the arbitrary normalization of a dependent variable, whereas LIML treats all endogenous variables included in an equation. TSLS has been criticized on these grounds, but it may be argued that this is a desirable rather than an undesirable facet of TSLS since normalization rules are usually present in practice, as indeed they should be if the equation is based on formal theoretical grounds rather than an intuitive idea that certain variables are connected. These normalization rules are thus in a real sense a part of the specification of the model, so the model is not completely specified unless each endogenous variable appears (at least implicitly) as a dependent variable. This is closely connected with the concept of autonomy, in that relationships of a model should as far as possible be directly causal, for this implies an explicit dependent variable. Computationally the limited information methods are relatively straightforward, though of the two considered TSLS is the simpler since LIML is complicated by the iterative procedure required to find the smallest root k.

OLS estimators are robust in the sense that their properties are not greatly affected by the type of phenomena being considered, though as these properties are not on the whole desirable for simultaneous systems this is of limited relevance. OLS is however the most simple method computationally.

Alternatives

Before deciding on a method for estimating the parameters of a simultaneous structure it is relevant to examine whether the structural parameters are needed at all (it is possible that the reduced form parameters might suffice), and whether a simultaneous system is required.

If only the reduced form parameters of the model were required OLS might provide a suitable method, for the difficulties associated with OLS when endogenous variables are treated as independent now disappear. However, if lagged endogenous variables are included among the predetermined variables then OLS is in general still biased, and even in the cases where it is unbiased is less efficient (asymptotically) than estimates of the reduced form derived from consistent estimates of the structural parameters. Thus it would appear to be preferable to estimate the structural parameters first by some simultaneous method even when only the reduced form is required—as in forecasting; indeed Christ [2] suggests that this may be true even where OLS estimators of the structure are better than simultaneous estimates of the structure. However, the overriding argument for the use of the structural form in this model is that its purpose is the understanding of the underlying forces, which requires a knowledge of the structure, not merely of the reduced form.

The model is essentially simultaneous, and illustrates to some extent the interdependence of the economic system. It has often been argued, for example by Wold, that this is a misrepresentation of economic forces, which are more validly interpreted as forming a causal chain, so that one variable only affects other variables in a stepwise and unilateral fashion. Such a sysem is termed recursive, and may be represented in the form

$$y_1 = z_1 + \omega_1$$

$$\beta_{21}y_1 + y_2 = z_2 + \omega_2$$

$$\cdot$$
$$\cdot$$
$$\cdot$$

$$\beta_{g1}y_1 + \beta_{g2}y_2 + \ldots + y_g = z_g + \omega_g \quad ,$$

where the z_i are linear combinations of the x_i, and where no current disturbance is correlated with any past disturbance and the variance-covariance matrix of the current disturbances is diagonal. The equations of such a system may be estimated seriatim by OLS, for OLS will produce consistent estimates where there are no independent endogenous variables, and these may be eliminated consecutively. If such a system were applicable, consistent full information estimates of the parameters could readily be obtained by OLS, so it is relevant to inquire whether the assumptions made by such a system are likely to be fulfilled.

The first assumption is that the coefficient matrix B is triangular (in the way illustrated), which implies that all causation takes place sequentially in time. For arbitrary small finite time periods this may be true, but in practice data almost invariably consists of averages over 'long' periods, when the model is in effect a simultaneous approximation to an underlying recursive model; in which case it should be estimated as fits the form it is, rather than the one it approximates.

The second assumption, that there is no serial correlation in the disturbances, is unlikely to be satisfied in practice. This applies especially to short time periods, when the diagonality of B is most likely, for then a shock engendered by a variable omitted from the equation (and part of the justifica-tion for a disturbance term is that not all relevant variables can be included in practice) is likely to be present for more than one time period.

Similarly, the assumption that the variance-covariance matrix is diagonal, or that there is no correlation between disturbances in different equations, is unlikely to be satisfied, for omitted variables or random shocks are likely to affect more than one included variable, and thus in general the residual in more than one equation.

Thus as a recursive system requires the satisfaction of three unlikely assumptions to be valid, a simultaneous system is retained, though this may be interpreted as an approximation to the underlying causal chains.

An alternative, suggested by Fisher [1], is the block recursive system, which is similar to a fully recursive system but requires the diagonality of a matrix whose elements are matrices of the parameters of the endogenous variables in parts of the system. This implies that the model is divisible into blocks, which though involving simultaneous relations between their constituent variables, are themselves only recursive. Since such a system still requires the choice of a method for estimating the parameters in each block simultaneously, and since it would not be logically plausible to divide this model into blocks other than by industry (and because of the nature of the links between industries such blocks could not be arranged recursively), this compromise is not pursued.

To summarize the two extreme methods, FIML seriously lacks robustness and is awkward computationally for large systems, while OLS is inconsistent and also apparently lacks any redeeming small sample properties; both are therefore discarded, leaving the choice (among the methods being considered), between LIML and TSLS. Many models are estimated by one of these methods, usually LIML, at first, then various equations are estimated by the other method if they do not appear acceptable. Such a procedure is undesirable methodologically, for it uses a priori considerations to reject an estimated equation, and assumes that the deficiency must be in the estimation method rather than in the specification (though more rational discrimination on the basis of the value of the smallest root k is possible). Conversely, it will accept an estimated equation if it conforms with (possibly false) a priori ideas, when this may have been caused by an incorrect specification combined with one of the presumed deficiencies in the estimation method. If an estimation method is to be relied on if it produces results which conform to a priori ideas then it should be relied on when it does not; if it is not relied on then a more acceptable method should be sought.

TSLS

The estimation method used is that of TSLS. This choice is based on the various facets discussed above, the deciding factor being the instability of LIML when k is in a (realistic) critical range, and the associated point of its being a k-class estimator with a stochastic k—an acceptable property usually but not consistently. It is used for all estimates, though where an equation is just identified this would be equivalent to LIML, and where it is already in its reduced form it is equivalent to OLS.

The main stages of the TSLS method are now examined from the viewpoint of understanding the computation procedure written for this study. For simplicity, and with no loss of generality, only the first equation of the model is considered, that is

$$\beta_{11} y_1 + \ldots \beta_{1g*} y_{g*} + \gamma_{11} x_1 + \ldots \gamma_{1h*} x_{h*} = \omega_1 .$$

This may be normalized on y_1 to obtain

$$y_1 = \beta_{12}^0 y_2 + \ldots \beta_{1g*}^0 y_{g*} + \gamma_{11}^0 x_1 + \ldots \gamma_{1h*}^0 x_{h*} + \omega_1 \ ,$$

where

$$\beta_{12}^0 = -\beta_{12}/\beta_{11} \ ,$$

and so on. Now define Y^* as the $n \times (g^* - 1)$ matrix of observations on the explanatory variables, so that $Y \equiv [y_1, Y^*]$ (the partitioned matrix), and X^* as the $n \times h^*$ matrix of observations on the predetermined variables in the equation; the associated parameter vectors β^* and γ^* are defined similarly, and the subscript is omitted from y_1 and ω_1. The equation now has the form

$$y = Y^* \beta^* + X^* \gamma^* + \omega \ .$$

The method of TSLS avoids the difficulties brought about by the correlation between ω and the variables in y^* by replacing the latter by its estimate as given by its OLS regression on all the predetermined variables, X. The basic OLS result gives this estimate as

$$\hat{Y}^* = X(X'X)^{-1} X'Y^* \ ,$$

so replacing Y^* by this in the equation gives

$$y = [X(X'X)^{-1} X'Y^*, X^*] (\beta^*, \gamma^*) + \omega \ .$$

Now applying OLS to this equation, again using the OLS result, gives the TSLS parameter estimates

$$(\hat{\beta}^*, \hat{\gamma}^*) = (Z'Z)^{-1} Z'y$$

where

$$Z = [X(X'X)^{-1} X'Y^*, X^*] \ .$$

The error of estimate ϵ is the difference between the estimated and true values of the parameters,

$$\epsilon \equiv (\hat{\beta}^*, \hat{\gamma}^*) - (\beta^*, \gamma^*) = (Z'Z)^{-1} Z' \omega$$

(using the above results). It may be shown that

$$\lim_{T \to \infty} E \, T \epsilon \epsilon' = \sigma^2 (Z'Z)^{-1} \ ,$$

which matrix is defined to be the asymptotic variance-covariance matrix for the estimators. In this expression σ^2 is the (unknown) variance of ω. It is replaced then by its estimate, which is usually taken to be the sum of squares of the observed residuals (that is of $\delta \equiv y - \hat{y}$) divided by the relevant number of degrees of freedom, that is $T - g^* - h^* + 1$. The asymptotic standard error of a parameter is readily derived from the principal diagonal of this matrix, being the square root of the relevant diagonal element.

The purpose of the above discusssion is solely to illustrate the main stages of the method in order to derive some efficient computational procedure, and so the results are not in their most usual form. A full treatment is not given as this may be found in many sources originating from Theil. Proofs that the estimates exist (that is that $Z'Z$ is nonsingular) if and only if the equation is identified, that the variance-covariance matrix is as claimed, and that the estimators have the asymptotic properties of consistency, normality, and efficiency are also given by Theil.

Appraisal

The appraisal of the estimates of the parameters of a model, as opposed to the appraisal of the whole model, is based on their actual values, and on the variances of these. The estimated values of the parameters should agree with a priori reasoning, and also with any available external empirical information. The exact variances of the parameter estimates are not known, only the approximate (asymptotic) variances, but these may be considered as the best estimates of the true variances and used to evaluate the confidence placed on the estimates of individual parameters in the standard way (using the t- or F-tests), as long as their approximate nature is recalled.

Confidence in the process whereby the estimates and their variances are derived will depend on the absence of serious multicollinearity and serial correlation of the disturbances. Both may be tested for; the former from an examination of the simple and multiple correlation coefficients among the predetermined variables, and the latter from the familiar measure of serial correlation of observed residuals (δ_t) that is

$$\sum_{t=2}^{T} (\delta_t - \delta_{t-1})^2 / \sum_{t=1}^{T} \delta_t^2 \ .$$

The overall goodness of fit may be measured by the standard error of estimate, that is the square root of the variance of the observed residuals, though this measure depends on the size of the dependent variable; it is thus useful for evaluating one form of an equation relative to another form, but not absolutely. Deflating this by the mean of the dependent variable is of little use if this may be near zero, and deflating by the variance merely produces a figure analogous to the familiar multiple correlation coefficient (R^2) in the single equation case (in fact $1 - R^2$). Thus if an absolute measure is required R^2 may be useful in the single equation case, though its meaning is not clear for a simultaneous model; indeed Christ [2, p. 519] shows that it is 'of no value as an indicator of the usefulness of a structural equation.' Basmann, in drawing attention to this misuse, defines R^2 as

$$1 - (\text{residual variance}) / (\text{total variance}) \ ,$$

and shows that it is misleading in that it may well be low (or even negative) without compromising the degree of confidence to be placed in the equation. This is illustrated by postulating a two equation supply and demand cobweb model, and showing that if the supply function is inelastic and has a residual with a low variance (relative to the demand function), then the measure of R^2 may well be negative. It is further shown that even for evaluating a reduced form equation this statistic is severely compromised by the fact that its probability distribution depends in a complex manner on the structural coefficients.

Basmann however only focuses on half of the problem, for in the single equation case R^2 may be equivalently defined as

$$(\text{explained variance}) / (\text{total variance}) \ .$$

Writing the model as

$$y = x + \omega$$

where x is a composite of all explanatory variables, the equivalence follows from the identity

$$\text{var}(y) = \text{var}(x) + \text{var}(\omega)$$

or

$$1 - \frac{\text{var}(\omega)}{\text{var}(y)} = \frac{\text{var}(x)}{\text{var}(y)} \ .$$

In general however,

$$\text{var}(y) = \text{var}(x) + \text{var}(\omega) + 2\text{cov}(x, \omega)$$

and $\text{cov}(x, \omega)$ is only zero in the single equation model, that is where no endogenous variables (correlated with ω) are included in x. Thus in general the two measures of R^2 are not equivalent. Denoting the former by R_0^2 and the latter by R_1^2, it is clear that

$$R_0^2 - R_1^2 = 2\text{cov}(x, \omega) / \text{var}(y) ,$$

that is the difference between the two measures is twice the covariance divided by the total variance. This suggests the possibility of a compromise measure, R_*^2, which includes the covariance divided by the total variance only once, that is

$$R_*^2 = R_0^2 - \text{cov}(x, \omega) / \text{var}(y) = R_1^2 + \text{cov}(x, \omega) / \text{var}(y)$$

or

$$R_*^2 = 1 - (\text{var}(\omega) + \text{cov}(x, \omega)) / \text{var}(y) = (\text{var}(x) + \text{cov}(x, \omega)) / \text{var}(y) .$$

R_*^2 clearly is the mean of R_0^2 and R_1^2, so the three measures coincide when the covariance is zero. Of course this compromise measure is the average of two deficient measures, and thus can only be regarded as a guide, in particular it may be noted that this measure may be negative or exceed unity, though such occurrences would appear to be very rare. It is however used here as there is no simple alternative and it may well be of some use if its deficiencies are recognized.

Sample

The data available consists of 44 time series observations on each variable. If the model is to be tested for prediction it is important to reserve some of these observations for this purpose—otherwise one introduces spurious accuracy. It has been argued, by Christ [2, p. 547] for example, that 'there is nothing that can be learned by saving some data for testing predictions that cannot also be learned by estimating on the basis of all the available data and examining all the residuals'; thus prediction only fills its role of the acid test of a model where it concerns a completely new set of data, with which the investigator is unfamiliar when the model is chosen. This represents an ideal: that the investigator cannot completely isolate himself from history while it is occurring, and thus implicitly uses information from the prediction period in formulating the model. In practice, the more standard approach is acceptable (and is in fact later adopted by Christ [2]), for if accuracy of prediction is to be assessed it is necessary either to save some of the immediately available data for prediction or to wait until more becomes available.

Thus part of the available data is reserved for prediction, and apart from being examined to determine the best method of making all the data compatible, is ignored until the estimated model is tested. Reserving the earlier part of the time period might have been preferable in that it would have meant that the estimated model was based on the most recent data, but, for a few variables (four), isolated observations preceding the main sample period are needed for initial values where those variables are lagged, so the latter part is reserved for prediction. This part consists of four more observations, which is the minimum required for a reasonable assessment of a quarterly model. This minimum is not exceeded as it is more appropriate to test rather cursorily a model built from a sound base than to investigate more thoroughly a model with weaker foundations. The sample is, then, the 36 observations of 1957 through 1965.

Block Structure

An immediate practical problem is that of insufficient degrees of freedom in the reduced form, for there are only 36 observations, but a substantially larger number of predetermined variables (because of nonlinearities and lagged values), so it is not possible to estimate the full reduced form parameters. Even if sufficient observations were available such estimation would be made very difficult because of multicollinearity, for it is improbable that a large number of (even predetermined) variables would not contain some highly collinear set. Thus estimation is by blocks—the model being divided into submodels each of which is estimated by TSLS using a subset of the available predetermined variables. It is apparent that there will be decreasing returns for each predetermined variable added, for the addition of a variable will in general increase the degree of multicollinearity somewhere, so the new variable adds little information; thus it may be reasonable to include only twenty or so predetermined variables. A block may consist of one equation, but such fineness is both laborious and unnecessary. In practice, blocks should consist of relatively highly interconnected equations; these may be chosen by inspection, which necessarily introduces a subjective element, or by an analysis of the causal structure as suggested by Fisher [1] —a process which may also prove valuable when the estimated model is to be solved. After the system has been divided into blocks a set of predetermined variables is chosen for each block. Clearly those appearing in the block must be included, but there may be some choice as regards others; here again choice may be subjective, though more rigorous methods are available. However, although this model is large it differs from other large models in that it is clearly divided into agent blocks, and so the problem of division into blocks does not arise more than formally. Blocks are agents and the number of predetermined variables in each agent's model is approximately the number required for each block, so these are the only predetermined variables taken into account.

Numerical Accuracy

It is difficult to comment on the numerical accuracy of the estimates produced, for hand computation of even one equation to a reasonable number of significant figures is out of the question. The degree of accuracy is of particular relevance where there is a significant degree of collinearity between variables (as there is here between some predetermined variables), since matrix inversion then involves division by the difference between two very similar figures. The problems have been investigated by Longley, who regresses employment in seven sectors, and total employment, on a set of six highly collinear independent variables, both by hand to eight significant figures and using a number of standard computer programs. The results are interesting: in many cases even the first significant figure of the computer estimated coefficients is incorrect, and some even have the wrong sign. A further test is provided by the aggregate regression, where the coefficients should be the sums of the individual coefficients, a condition which is rarely satisfied by the computer estimates. The main reason for the inaccuracy of most of these computer estimates is that the computers tend to have short word lengths (lsufficient to carry around eight digits), though a correspondingly large number of words in the store. The machine used for this study however has an unusually large word length (sufficient to carry around eleven digits), and a small store; this makes estimation awkward, yet more accurate. Longley's model (with appropriate scaling) was estimated by the OLS variant of the procedure used with encouraging results: all the parameter estimates were correct to the number of significant places given (that is three), and the aggregate coefficients were sums of their respective components. This provides no direct indication of the accuracy of the TSLS estimates, but is encouraging, for the TSLS program uses the same routines for matrix inversion (which is where inaccuracy is most likely to originate) and the same machine as the OLS version; however, the matrices are larger in the TSLS computations, and so are more likely to contain collinear variables.

5.2 PRODUCERS ESTIMATES

The parameter estimates that are produced by the estimation process are now examined, starting with those for the industry models; the estimates themselves are given in Appendix B. The discussion is an assessment and interpretation of the figures, emphasizing some interesting results, and is in no way a substitute for the Appendix—indeed the discussion should be interpreted in conjunction with the Appendix. A rigorous analysis of the implications of all the particular findings is beyond the scope of this study.

      The estimates presented are the results of estimating the theoretical outline industry model by TSLS for each of the ten industries, and making various modifications to this outline model in certain industries in the light of empirical evidence. In the discussion of Section 4.1 it was stressed that the function of the outline model is to express as far as possible the relations that apply to any industry, whatever the nature of its technology or state of competition, and that the main difference between industries would be the varying importance of certain factors, reflected in the different (possibly zero) values of the estimated coefficients. Thus little basic modification is necessary, and where this does occur the underlying reasons are readily apparent. In the interests of simplicity variables are removed from relationships if their coefficients are of virtually no statistical significance. This particularly aids clarity where they are, insignificantly, in a theoretically impossible range. The lowest level of significance of included variables is that where the coefficient is one-third of its standard error (in modulus)—a very liberal interpretation of significance.

The estimates of individual parameters may be assessed according to their actual values and their t-ratios; the complete equations may be assessed according to their standard errors of estimate, measure of serial correlation, and (tentatively) the goodness of fit—the statistic approximately analogous to the multiple correlation coefficient in the single equation case. The theoretical interpretation of these is standard or has been discussed above; it should however be noted that the goodness of fit statistic includes (in effect) the proportion of the variance explained by the seasonal terms. Numerically, the value of the t-ratio required for significance at the five percent level is approximately 2.0 (its exact value depends on the number of variables in the equation), and the value of the serial correlation of residuals is approximately 2.0; positive autocorrelation may be inferred from values less than 1.5 (again approximately, and at the five percent level of significance), and negative autocorrelation from values greater than 2.5. Outlying observations are those time periods for which the residual is of exceptionally large absolute size, such as would be expected to occur in only one percent of observations (assuming that the residuals are normally distributed), that is greater than 2.75 times the standard error of estimate. No mention is made of the seasonal or constant terms.

The individual stochastic equations are now discussed under the headings in which they were presented in Chapter 4. (There is of course no discussion of equations (8)-(10)).

Demand (1)

As it was indicated in Chapter 4 that this equation is virtually an identity, the estimates of its parameters require little discussion; as is to be expected these estimates appear very satisfactory. The intermediate demand variable is very significant, and appears to account for a reasonable proportion of total demand, this being lowest for industry n; it should be recalled, however, that this is defined in part by the dependent variable. It is clearly worthwhile including changes in stocks, for these are relevant for all industries but one (e), usually with reasonable significance. This is the only element of demand that is directly determined by the industry, though the industry's production decision may be influenced from within through its pricing decision. The final demand components are of reasonable importance, and are in general associated with the industries expected. There is only slight evidence of (positive) serial correlation of the residuals, and as is to be expected the goodness of fit statistic is everywhere extremely high. Two industries (p and o) each have the one (the same) outlying observation.

Supply (2)

This is essentially a linear production function which is used as a demand for labor function; the coefficients of both factors should of course be positive. The theoretical form proposed appears satisfactory, for with one exception both labor and adjusted capital are relevant for all industries, usually (the latter always) with reasonable significance. The overall goodness of fit is high, and there are no outlying observations; however, some serial correlation of residuals is present in most industries.

A linear function can only indicate approximate figures for marginal productivities. These are best interpreted from the average elasticities of output, since these are independent of the units used, and the units of output in different industries are not immediately comparable. These average elasticities, the average percentage change in output associated with a unit percentage change in the factor input, may be calculated by multiplying the relevant coefficients by the ratio of the mean of the factor series to that of the output series. As was indicated in Chapter 4, some implications of the main alternative formulation are also considered here—since the production function is a particularly important equation. These elasticities are therefore compared with the marginal productivities of factors as derived from the logarithmic function, modified by the incorporation of additive seasonal terms in the logarithmic form (and with no constraint on the sum of the two parameters); the modification is to facilitate comparison. This alternative form expressed in logarithms is thus

$$\log x = \alpha_1 \log l + \alpha_2 \log k_{-1} \, l/(l+u) + \gamma \ .$$

On the whole these elasticities indicate greatly varying degrees of economies of scale in different industries, but do not appear implausible given the approximate nature of the figures. The one exceptional figure is that for capital in industry **t**, which appears very large. This is perhaps understandable in view of the nature of the industry—with rationalization against a background of high excess capacity producing an increase in output (for a given labor force) with little addition to capital stock. In general the marginal productivities or output elasticities implied by the two forms of the equation correspond very closely. The largest difference occurs for labor in industry **e**; there is no immediately obvious explanation for this, for employment in this industry is not particularly volatile.

The one industry where both factors are not relevant is industry **c**, where labor appears completely insignificant. This is not a particularly surprising result considering the extreme capital intensiveness of this industry, and indeed an adequate production function is obtained by omitting labor, when capital remains very significant, producing a high goodness of fit, though serious serial correlation of residuals. However, this is clearly inadequate as a labor demand function, and leads to the first of the modifications to the outline model. The zero effect of output on the demand for labor is interpreted as the demand for labor being purely institutionally determined, or as all labor being overhead labor; this is formalized in the simple model

$$l = l_{-1} + \omega \ ,$$

that is that the demand for labor is last period's demand plus some purely random residual. Alternative relationships were considered, of which perhaps the most relevant was that more labor is not needed to increase output from a given amount of plant, but that more plant requires more (overhead) labor, that is

$$l = \alpha k_{-1} + \gamma \ .$$

But experiments indicated that the former model is as satisfactory, and so being simpler, this is adopted. This equation, which requires no estimation, thus replaces the outline supply equation in industry **c**; this leads to further necessary changes for this industry.

Stocks (3)

This equation combines an expectational accelerator with speculative motives; all coefficients should be positive, and that of the last period's change of stocks should be less than unity. The accelerator effect appears relevant in six industries, but price speculation appears somewhat more important, being relevant in all but two industries (**n**, understandably in view of the price series used, and **s**). The expectational approach appears to be valuable, the lagged change of stocks term being relevant for all industries but one (**f**), usually with reasonable significance. The goodness of fit is acceptable in view of the extremely volatile nature of the dependent variable, and except in industry **f** (which does not include the lagged change of stocks term) there is no evidence of any serial correlation of residuals. Three industries each have one (different) outlying observation.

It is apparent that the acceleration coefficients are all very small, and thus that the accelerator hypothesis in the form used here is not very important. However, this does not detract from the accelerator hypothesis in its general sense, for this simply relates desired stocks to anticipated sales, neither of which are observable. This model has attempted to allow for these unobservable values according to certain subsidiary hypotheses, but as these hypotheses are by their nature untestable, no firm contradiction of the basic accelerator hypothesis may be inferred, and only a certain doubt is thrown on this formulation—though unless some hypothesis is made about these unobservable values the basic accelerator theory is not meaningful.

The acceleration coefficient may be interpreted as the value of the change in stocks associated with a unit change in the value of sales over a unit time period; the dimension is thus that of time, and the coefficient could be interpreted as a crude indication of the 'payback period' if all stock formation were associated with the accelerator. The acceleration coefficient (in units of quarters of a year) is thus obtained by dividing the coefficient of the change in the index by the base of the index for the relevant industry; where the accelerator is relevant, its average value is approximately 0.5

Labor (4)

This equation expresses the supply of labor in terms of its relative remuneration and general availability; all coefficients should be positive, and those of aggregate labor and unemployment should sum to less than unity. Relative remuneration does not appear to be of great importance; it is relevant for all but three industries, but frequently with little significance. The two measures of general availability are important: with one exception aggregate labor is significant in all industries, and aggregate unemployment in half of the industries. The exception is industry **t**, which has uniquely experienced a steady decline in labor force over the period, and for which the availability of labor is clearly of little relevance. The overall performance of this equation is only moderate; goodness of fit is usually satisfactory, sometimes high, but all industries have significant positive serial correlation of residuals. There are two industries (**e** and **p**) with one (the same) outlying observation.

Again industry **c** needs revision, for if labor demand is determined institutionally, the supply of labor may be expected to contract at times when labor demand is relatively low and the expected value (in the statistical sense) of earnings for each member of the labor force is also low—though the expected value for those in employment remains high. Thus where employment or unemployment appears arbitrary (or is not determined through output) and does not directly affect the level of earnings (see equation 7), the level of relative earnings can only be taken as an indication of the attraction of the industry if it is weighted in some way to allow for the probability of those earnings not being received, that is of the worker being unemployed. This is clearly the case for industry **c**, for when no account of taken of this none of the three explanatory variables of the outline model appear relevant, yet when an additional variable l/u is included to take account of this they all become relevant and l/u is itself highly significant.

This is the first of the two changes to the basic industry model that require reestimation. The basic and modified estimated equations are presented here: the figures in parentheses under the coefficients are their t-ratios, SC is the serial correlation measure, GF is the goodness fit, and κ is a composite of the constant and seasonal terms (the modified equation is given here for ease of comparison—it is also given in Appendix B). The equations are

basic: $l + u = -19.5\ e\Sigma l/\Sigma el + 0.000237\ \Sigma l - 0.0409\ \Sigma u + \kappa; SC\ 0.4$
            (0.04) (0.0) (1.4) $GF\ 0.14$

modified: $l + u = $ $48.4\ e\Sigma l/\Sigma el + 0.0204\ \Sigma l + 0.174\ \Sigma u + 0.854\ l/u + \kappa; SC\ 0.8$
               (1.0) (2.7) (2.5) (3.2) $GF\ 0.44$

Other ways of incorporating this effect are possible, perhaps the most direct being the replacement of relative earnings $e\Sigma l/\Sigma el$, by its expected value, $el\Sigma l/(l + u)\ \Sigma el$, but this assumes that the income of those not employed would be zero, which is not the case if they receive unemployment compensation. Thus for industry c the labor equation at this stage is

$$l + u = \alpha_{41} e\Sigma l/\Sigma el + \alpha_{42}\Sigma l + \alpha_{43}\Sigma u + \alpha_{44} l/u + \gamma_4 \ .$$

An examination of this equation in conjunction with the labor demand equation suggests an important further change in the final model. This arises because the labor demand equation essentially determines l, which is a large part (about 98 percent) of the dependent variable $l + u$ of the labor supply equation. Thus a small inaccuracy in the solved values of l or $l + u$ would lead to a large inaccuracy in the solved value of u: for example if the true value of l and $l + u$ were 99 and 101 and the solved values were 101 and 99 respectively (that is each involving about 2 percent error), the solved value of u would be –2 instead of +2, which is clearly unacceptable—particularly as the inverse of u is used elsewhere (in equation 7). This is unavoidable if u is expressed as the difference between $l + u$ and l, which is the theoretically meaningful way. The modification adopted places a small arbitrary lower bound to the value of u, which is taken as a fraction η of the value of l. Defining

$$\tilde{l} + \tilde{u} = \alpha_{41} e\Sigma l/\Sigma el + \alpha_{42}\Sigma l + \alpha_{43}\Sigma u + \gamma_4$$

for all industries but c, and the corresponding expression (that is with the additional term $\alpha_{44} l/u$) for c, the final modified equation is

$$l + u = \max\{\tilde{l} + \tilde{u} \ , \ (1 + \eta)l\} \ .$$

(In practice, η is taken to be one percent.) It is apparent that this form is not differentiable; it may however be interpreted as an approximation to some true smoother function—if it is believed that reality is smooth. This (somewhat arbitrary) modification makes the equation more suitable for prediction. It is irrelevant in estimation as it happens that in the observed sample period $u > \eta l$ anyway, and for the same reason it is also irrelevant in equilibrium solutions; its introduction is necessary to ensure that at no disequilibrium state is any u nonpositive, which would otherwise occur. Other variables are not explicitly bounded as the implicit bounds of the structure are sufficient.

Investment (5)

The fixed investment equation may be considered a parallel to the inventory investment equation, determining investment by a combination of the expectational accelerator, profitability or liquidity, and desired stock or replacement motives. All coefficients except that of lagged capital stock (positive or

negative) should be positive and that of lagged investment should not exceed
unity. The acceleration principle appears to be of minor importance, being at all
relevant in only four industries and then with little significance. The profitability
or liquidity effect appears to be the basic determinant, being relevant for all
industries, usually significantly. The lagged capital term is relevant for all industries except one (**p**) but at slightly lower levels of significance; the coefficient
is positive in five of the nine relevant industries, indicating that the depreciation
or replacement effect outweighs the desired stock effect, the converse applying
in the other four. Expectations are very important, for the lagged investment
term is relevant in all industries except one (**o**), usually with very high significance. The goodness of fit is on the whole surprisingly high considering the
nature of the dependent variable, and there is no evidence of serial correlation
of residuals in any industry. Industry **n** has one outlying observation.

The implications of these estimates on the relatively small importance
of the accelerator are contrary to a number of findings, for example those of
Eisner, and are thus surprising—particularly so since the equation appears on the
whole to be satisfactory statistically. The remarks on the accelerator made
above, that the basic relation concerns two unobservable variables and that the
apparent failure of an observable extension may merely imply an incorrect
interpretation of this, apply equally here—so it is possible that for example the
wrong lag structure is being used.

A more fruitful explanation of the greater apparent importance of
profits than the accelerator concerns the prima facie similarity of the two
motives. As Eisner [p. 173] shows, 'with almost any reasonable production
function, one should expect increases in demand sooner or later to generate
capital expenditures, and profits to be associated with capital expenditures only
to the extent that they themselves were associated with the pressure of demand
on capacity [so] capital expenditures would be associated with profits per se
only where imperfections of capital markets were likely to be significant.' The
first part of this statement suggests that profits are in general relevant only as a
proxy for other factors (notably capacity utilization), and it is likely that some
part of the profits variable included here is important only as a proxy for other
factors connected with the acceleration motive which must for practical reasons
be excluded. The latter part of the statement is also important, for imperfections in the capital market are widely recognized, and indeed form the basis of
financial capitalism. Thus only some part of the profits variable is likely to reflect
the relevance of profits per se; unfortunately, information from outside the
scope of this study would be required to identify the sizes of these two parts.
The immediate inference that the profits effect is more important than the
accelerator effect is not necessarily refuted, but may be qualified to be relevant
only when serious imperfections in the capital market exist, which apparently
applies in the environment of this study.

The actual values of the acceleration coefficients are small, as are those for inventory investment; again it appears that even when the accelerator is absolutely significant it is of relatively small importance. It seems that the fixed investment accelerators are smaller on the whole than those for inventory investment, though there is not sufficient evidence to establish this more than very tentatively. This would however be a somewhat surprising result in view of the observable large differences in the total amounts of fixed and inventory capital required for the same output, though these amounts indicate the average rather than the marginal figures, which need not (despite the development of the concept) be assumed equal. The main inference that may be drawn from the relative and absolute sizes of these figures is that the accelerator is of marginal importance here.

Price (6)

The price formation equation is based on a modified markup process, where the coefficients of the two cost terms should clearly be positive, and that of the level of stocks relative to output in the last period negative. As was mentioned above, this equation does not apply to industry n, where it is replaced by a definition which states that the price in this industry is that for the economy, which is thus equivalent to the average of the prices of the other industries, or the price for m.

In all industries where the basic equation does apply the price of materials is of prime importance, being relevant for all industries with very high levels of significance; it should be recalled however that this is defined in part by the dependent variable. Unit labor costs appear to be of less importance, being relevant in five of the nine industries with only moderate significance, while the pressure of demand term is only relevant for four industries, with slightly less significance. With one exception, the overall performance of the equation is good, with high goodness of fit and usually only small evidence of serial correlation of residuals; the exception is again industry c, where goodness of fit is fairly low and there is serious positive autocorrelation of residuals. Industry e has one outlying observation.

The estimates of this equation are substantially as would be expected, and are not discussed further.

Earnings (7)

The earnings equation expresses the rate of change of earnings as a function of four separate factors, each of which should have a positive effect. Rather surprisingly, unemployment does not appear to be very important, being relevant in only half of the industries, and then with no great significance. The rates of change of output and of profits are each relevant in four industries, at only moderate levels of significance, and for no industries are both relevant; this suggests that they are to some extent substitutes, and in fact these variables are significantly collinear, despite their different time periods. The rate of change of consumer prices is relevant for half of the industries. Closer investigation shows that seasonal factors are of particular importance, possibly reflecting the annual nature of the wage component in earnings; ideally more of this seasonal pattern should be explained, but no better simple formulation is apparent. This applies particularly to industry **v**, for which the equation is (perhaps not surprisingly) particularly poor, and where the seasonal factors appear to be the only relevant factors. The equation for this industry is thus purely artificial or empirical: this is clearly undesirable but is retained as no simple theoretically and statistically satisfactory alternative seems available.

Industry **c** again forms a special case, for as is to be expected in the light of the discussion on employment and unemployment in this industry, the equation incorporating industry unemployment is very inadequate, but becomes slightly more acceptable when industry unemployment is replaced by aggregate unemployment. In both cases unemployment is the only relevant term, and the equation is not particularly satisfactory. This is the second of the two modifications to the basic model requiring reestimation; the basic and modified estimated equations (in the same format as in the first case—equation 4) are

basic: $\quad e/e_{-1} = -0.112/u + \kappa; SC\ 3.0$
$\qquad\qquad (0.0) \qquad\qquad GF\ 0.21$

modified: $\quad e/e_{-1} = 5.96/\Sigma u + \kappa;\ SC\ 3.0$
$\qquad\qquad\ (0.5) \qquad\qquad GF\ 0.23$

On the whole this equation is acceptable in most industries; goodness of fit is satisfactory, and there is only slight evidence of (negative) serial correlation of residuals. Industry **p** has one outlying observation.

The implication of these estimates on the importance of unemployment is at first sight contradictory to most work on the relation between unemployment and inflation. The superiority of industry to aggregate unemployment, the use of the reciprocal of unemployment, and the choice of lag were discussed in Chapter 4. The basic difference between this equation and most others is the use of earnings rather than wages as the dependent variable, and the difference in results may be tentatively ascribed to this. This would be compatible with the hypothesis that wages are determined primarily by the level of unemployment while the excess of earnings over wages is determined by other factors, and that the variance of the latter is large enough to swamp the former. As figures for wage rates are not used in the model this hypothesis cannot be tested here, but would appear plausible; indeed the decision to omit wages depended in part on their arbitrary, and static, nature relative to earnings. This effect might be expected to be emphasized in a quarterly model where the level of wages might not change for three quarters (wage bargaining being predominantly an annual process), and particularly so in a disaggregated model where annual wage changes in individual industries cannot through aggregation produce a series with more movement from quarter to quarter. However, this explanation must remain tentative in the absence of further information.

Alternative Profits

Profits in this equation are determined by sales, which should have a positive coefficient, and by two other variables whose coefficients may be positive or negative. As expected, sales are significant in all industries; both unit labor costs and lagged sales are relevant in all industries but **f**. The overall goodness of fit is high, and there is little evidence of serial correlation of residuals; there are no outlying observations.

This equation has some implications for the degrees of competition in the industries. In competitive industries high sales would mean more firms, and would therefore have a modified effect on profits; more specifically, the effect of new entrants to the industry would be represented by a negative correlation of profits with past sales, but unit labor costs would be positively correlated with profits. In more monopolistic industries sales would be important with past sales less so, and unit labor costs would be negatively correlated with profits.

Thus a primarily competitive industry is associated with a positive coefficient for unit labor costs and a significant negative lagged sales term, whereas a primarily monopolistic industry is associated with a negative coefficient for unit labor costs and no (or an insignificant positive) lagged sales term. The industries may thus be classified in two ways which are reasonably internally consistent, agreeing in seven industries and disagreeing in two (unit labor costs are not relevant either way for industry **v** and thus do not give it any classification). This identifies five industries (**n, c, e, v, t**) as being primarily competitive, three (**s, h, p**) primarily monopolistic, and two (**f, o**) indeterminate. It is not clear how accurate these classifications are, for the calculation of concentration ratios or other independent measures is outside the scope of this study, and the industry disaggregation does not readily correspond with that used in other work on competitive structures. (Since this equation does not appear in the real model, but only in the alternative model, the estimates discussed here are omitted from Appendix B.)

Summary

The overall impression derived from the estimates is that the theoretical outline industry model is, with certain exceptions, reasonably satisfactory; when these exceptions are allowed for by the changes suggested it becomes acceptable for further testing by prediction. These changes fall into three categories. Firstly, there is the change due to the lack of data, that is in the price equation in industry **n**. Secondly, there are the more fundamental changes to the model for industry **c** which are occasioned by the unimportance of labor (at the margin) in this industry's production process; these are the replacement of the output related labor demand function by an institutional relation, the allowance for unemployment in the labor supply function, and the replacement of industry by aggregate unemployment in the earnings equation. Thirdly, there is the modification of the labor equation in all industries to make it more suitable for prediction in a simultaneous equation context.

As part of the purpose of this study is the formulation of an outline model which would describe any industry, the need for these changes is a prima facie criticism. The main purpose of the empirical model however is to produce industry models accurate enough to be combined into a reasonable whole, and the changes made have acceptable theoretical bases: the first change is trivial, the second changes are all interrelated and are made necessary by the observed unimportance of labor in industry c, and the third applies an important logical constraint (albeit in a rather arbitrary way).

It is relevant that for the 78 (that is $10 \times 8 - 2$) estimated industry equations, each involving 36 observations, there are only 10 outlying observations (as would be expected in only one percent of the observations if the residuals were normally distributed), whereas approximately 28 could be expected. Further, five of these ten are for the same observation (63.1); it did not seem worthwhile, and would have been of doubtful validity, to reestimate the model without this observation. This suggests that the residuals are not normally distributed, but are subnormally kurtotic, which contradicts one of the ideal assumptions of the estimation process. This effect is in an acceptable direction, for the assumption of normality in such a case would tend to produce larger standard errors (of parameters and estimate) than the true values, so greater confidence may be placed on the inferences from the values obtained, as the true values will tend to be smaller.

5.3 CONSUMERS ESTIMATES

The estimates of the final model are now examined—in less detail than those of the industry models because they have fewer problems (all equations fit very well), and also because they enter less into the overall interaction. Naturally, all the introductory comments of the preceding section continue to apply.

Consumption (i)

Consumption is primarily determined by disposable labor income, which is of prime importance of all categories of consumption except that of v. The short run marginal propensities to consume (with respect to disposable labor income only) are given by the coefficients of this term, and the long run propensities, that is the propensities where consumers are no longer adjusting their expenditures, are given by reformulating the equations with current consumption equal to last period's consumption. These figures however have little theoretical meaning, as property income may also be spent on consumption—the equations are only based on the concept of disposable labor income for simplicity. Relative prices are important for all categories except, as might be expected, that of **f**, and the expectational factor provided by the lagged consumption term is important for all categories except that of **t**. The overall goodness of fit is very high and there is no evidence of significant serial correlation of residuals.

Consumer Prices (ii)

These are determined by a markup process from wholesale prices with allowance for purchase taxes. As is to be expected, wholesale prices are always very important; tax rates are important for all categories except that of **o**. The overall goodness of fit is very high except for the category of **v**, but there is definite serial correlation of residuals.

Imports (iii)

Both categories of imports depend significantly on total factor income, both with significant distributed lag effects. Goodness of fit is high, with slight evidence of positive serial correlation of residuals.

Exports (iv)

Both categories of exports depend very significantly on the level of world trade, with the expectational factor being relevant for that of **n** but not for that of **m**. Goodness of fit is high and the residuals are reasonably serially independent.

Summary

There is little to be said about the estimates of the consumer's model other than they are all very accurate (in the goodness of fit sense), and that the model therefore fulfills its purpose of completing the partition of economic activity. The later discussion will bear this accuracy in mind, and concentrate on the industry models.

Part III

Analysis

Chapter Six

Partial Equilibrium

The second part of this study developed a tool for the quantitative analysis of general economic equilibrium: that is, applied the abstract concepts of a model developed in Chapter 2 to the economy under consideration, estimating any unknown parameters by using methods of statistical inference from observed reality. In this final part this tool is used: that is the estimated model is 'solved' to obtain some quantitative static and dynamic properties of the system; in the abstract notation of Chapter 2 the first are given by the properties of the function $F(x)$, mapping characteristics or exogeneous variables x to the corresponding equilibrium states or endogeneous variables y, and the second by the properties of the sequence

$$(y, f(y), f(f(y)), \dots)\qquad ,$$

in particular whether this has a limit. (Part III continues to use the abstract notation of Part I, and does not mix this with the concrete notation of Part II.)

In outline, the discussion starts with the fully specified model f, or $(f^1, \dots f^n)$, from Part II, and considers the action rule f^i of each agent individually, to obtain some information on the partial equilibrium properties of the model (Chapter 6). This information is then used to consider the general equilibrium properties of the model: firstly stability, and then using the results of this, comparative statics (Chapter 7). Finally some applications are suggested and some conclusions offered (Chapter 8).

Since the general equilibrium comparative statics of the model are to be investigated it is not obvious why one should be interested in the partial. The main reason for this, besides a minor one noted in Chapter 7, is that in empirical models such as this the validity, at a practical level, of both general equilibrium comparative statics and dynamics requires that the underlying models be in some sense accurate. As will be seen, this in turn depends on the partial equilibrium comparative statics, or partial solutions. This is the subject matter of the present chapter. This commences with some general remarks on the theory of assessment of empirical models and the evaluation of solutions, then presents and interprets some results; finally some of the technical problems involved in actually solving the models are mentioned.

6.1 ASSESSMENT THEORY

Before one can learn much from the solutions of the models one must first consider how to interpret these; this is done now.

Prediction

Assessment of an empirical model may be either predictive or non-predictive, the latter typically being based on the information contained in the sample set. Since this model, as most models, is derived from the concurrent development of theory and observation, and as observation is the sample set, the model itself embodies the information one seeks to confront it with. It follows that the usual processes of statistical inference will cease to apply. If indeed they are used then bias must result: it is clear that the assessment arrived at will be too optimistic. To obtain a more acceptable assessment, then, one must incorporate new information, that is turn to predictive assessment.

The term 'prediction' is used to refer to statements about elements known to occur in the sample space which have not been taken into account in the specification of the predicting function, or model (though strictly speaking the elements may be repetitions of elements which have been taken into account). In this sense prediction does not involve time, so may concern elements labelled 'past' as well as those labelled 'future.' Since one may consider the stochastic model as a function from the space of values of the exogenous variables to the space of probability distributions over the values of the endogenous variables, say $\widetilde{F}: X \to \widetilde{Y}$, one may think of a prediction, relative to an actual value, as the pair $(y, \widetilde{F}(x))$—where the exogenous variables $x \in X$ and the endogenous variables $y \in Y$ are observed.

A theme which will become apparent throughout this part of the study is that while the abstract investigation of general equilibrium may fruitfully use large amounts of information, that is information from dimensionless or large dimensional spaces, the quantitative investigation may not. Indeed 'quantitative' is usually taken to imply 'numbers,' that is elements of the real line. One will, therefore, frequently be forced to disregard much of the information available, or to condense it into smaller dimensional spaces—typically the real line, or a small dimensional cartesian product of this. This must necessarily be arbitrary, in the sense of being specified by some outside criterion. But this need be no criticism, and indeed the most valuable part of quantitative economics may consist of the specification of suitable, that is intuitively acceptable and interpretable, condensations.

In particular, here one must condense the space of probability distributions into a space more naturally comparable with that of actual values, that is obtain point predictions. Typically the expectations operator $E: \widetilde{Y} \rightarrow Y$ is used as a condensation, so the prediction reduces to the pair $(y, E \cdot \widetilde{F}(x))$, where $E \cdot F$ is the composite mapping, or more simple $(y, F(x))$. In other words, the prediction consists of the actual values of endogenous variables together with the expected value point estimate of these.

Evaluation

Given a prediction $(y, F(x))$, it must be evaluated. One would like to say it was a good prediction if the point estimate $F(x)$ was close to the actual value y. This raises two problems: firstly, how to measure the distance from $F(x)$ to y, and secondly, when is this small? Again neither point raises any problem in abstract analysis, as Y is naturally a metric space, so one may choose any metric on Y for the distance, and say this is small if this tends to zero in some sense. In a quantitative analysis however there are more serious problems of interpretation. The actual value of a distance is naturally difficult to interpret in such a space, and this difficulty is compounded by the fact that the dimensions, or components, of the space are themselves measured in different units—for example tons, pounds (sterling), men, and so on. It may then be preferable to condense the information in a different way, and instead of choosing a metric on Y, choose one or two particularly important or representative components of y, say y_h, and record separately the closeness of the point estimate $(F(x))_h$, denoted F_h, to the actual value y_h of this component; distance here is readily measurable, without difficulties of interpretation, by the absolute value metric.

The question of when the distance is small clearly cannot be answered without regard to what is being estimated. Thus one cannot merely fix a number arbitrarily, but instead must fix some rule arbitrarily, that is propose an alternative model, but an alternative which is fundamentally different to the prior model. The way in which it differs must depend on what the model is claiming: this model essentially rests on the belief that economic activity is the result of individual optimization, so an appropriate alternative model would be purely mechanical, that is a so-called 'naive model.'

The questions of condensing predictions to point predictions, finding some suitable measure of the accuracy of these, and determining some suitable method of saying when this is small, are now discussed for this specific model.

To arrive at a point prediction the specification is made that the random disturbance term in each equation assumes its expected value, that is zero. This of course means that the point prediction $F(x)$ is not the expected value of the distribution $\widetilde{F}(x)$, for not only is the model nonlinear, but also the variance-covariance matrix of parameter estimates cannot be expected to be diagonal, so that even if the model were linear one would not have this expected value, because of the neglect of these covariances. Nevertheless, the expected value of $\widetilde{F}(x)$ is by no means the only reasonable candidate for a point prediction, and this alternative (which might be expected to be close to this) is readily interpretable. Further, it is not possible to compute the expected value of $\widetilde{F}(x)$ here, because the limited information estimation method used in obtaining the structure does not take account of the specification of any of the equations in the model other than the one being estimated, so that covariances between estimates of parameters in different structural equations are not available.

By assuming that all disturbances are zero a more rigorous assessment of the model is made, for this ignores information on the autoregressive structure of the disturbances. This is desirable for analysis; if however one simply wanted to forecast one would naturally use this information.

In order to measure the accuracy, or equivalently error, of predictions a metric is not defined on Y, but instead two particularly important components of Y are considered. These are (for the producing agents) the levels of output, y_x, representing the overall scale of the agent, and of profits, y_z, into which each other variable y_h enters with a weight, in the sense of dy_z/dy_h, which is perhaps appropriate. (It might be noted that since the variables y_h are interdependent it is not implausible that each of these components is in fact a metric on Y—though not equivalent metrics.)

The absolute value norm is then used, so the error of the prediction (y_h, F_h) is measured by $|F_h - y_h|$. However, to reduce problems of comparability this is represented as a proportion, that is as the proportional prediction error,

$$e_h = |F_h - y_h|/y_h \qquad (h = x, z)$$

(it happens that there are no problems of definition). The error of the prediction $(y, F(x))$ is thus measured by the pair (e_x, e_z).

Now a further problem arises which was not apparent in the more abstract discussion. This is that there are not one but m such pairs to evaluate—one for each producing agent. Naturally this information is used, but since for quantitative results to be interpretable they should be of small dimension, it is also helpful to condense this $2m$ dimensional information into something smaller. Denoting the agent by a superscript, the m-tuple $(e_h^1, \ldots e_h^m)$ is a point in R^m, where each dimension is measured independently of units, so this may be reasonably condensed by taking the euclidean norm, to obtain

$$E_h = [(e_h^1)^2 + \ldots + (e_h^m)^2]^{1/2} \qquad (h = x, z).$$

In other words, E_h is simply the root-mean-square proportional error of prediction of y_h over all sectors. The overall error of prediction is then measured by the pair (E_x, E_z).

To decide when this measure of the error of prediction is small one must, as suggested, specify an arbitrary rule rather than an arbitrary number for comparison. This rule, or naive model, represents the alternative hypothesis that the path of the economy is simply determined by some internal auto-regressive structure. Since many such structures are possible the three simplest are specified, then, for each possible prediction individually, the most accurate of these three is taken. This of course generates an improper prediction model, because its prediction of y cannot be made without knowledge of y. Since the real model is compared with this, this merely means that comparison becomes more stringent, which is quite acceptable; indeed it is important to note that taking the best of the three naive models for each prediction (that is of variable in each time period) individually, rather than the best over some set, makes the comparison really quite severe.

The three naive structures specified are the following. Firstly, that the prediction of y_h ($h = x, z$) in period t is given by the value of y_h in the preceding period, so the expected change is zero; this gives

$$y_h^*(t) = y_h(t - 1),$$

with associated proportional prediction error

$$e_h^* = |y_h^* - y_h|/y_h.$$

Secondly, that the expected absolute change is constant, or

$$y_h^{**}(t) = 2y_h(t - 1) - y_h(t - 2),$$

with associated error e_h^{**} defined analogously to e_h^*. And thirdly, that the expected proportional change (it happens that there are no problems of definition) is constant, or

$$y_h^{***}(t) = y_h(t - 1)/y_h(t - 2),$$

again with associated error e_h^{***} defined analogously to e_h^*.

Now in parallel with the actual model an overall measure of the error of prediction of the three components of the naive model is defined by the root-mean-square error of prediction over all agents, that is by

$$E_h^* = [(e_h^{*1})^2 + \ldots + (e_h^{*m})^2]^{1/2},$$

with analogous measures E_h^{**} and E_h^{***}. The measure of error of prediction of the (complete) naive model is then given by

$$E_h^0 = \min\{E_h^*, E_h^{**}, E_h^{***}\}.$$

The measure of the error or prediction of the actual model is thus said to be small if it is less than of the naive model, that is if $E_h < E_h^0$ $(h = x, z)$.

Forecasting

One now has a method for deciding whether the model is accurate in prediction, and thus of assessing the model. It is however important to clarify the meaning of this assessment, which is based on the predictive performance of each of the individual agents' models, say $f^i\colon X \to Y^i$. Now variables in the set X are not all purely exogenous: some are the link variables, that is variables exogenous to agent i but endogenous to some other agent j, and therefore to the whole model. Thus although all the individual models f^i comprise the complete model F, the satisfactory predictive power of each f^i does not imply the satisfactory predictive power of F. This however is acceptable here, as this chapter is concerned only with the partial equilibrium solutions, where the purpose is to assess the validity of the submodels as determining the partial equilibrium behavior of the individual agents.

It may be of secondary interest to examine the accuracy of the submodels in a more absolute sense, or of pure forecasts, that is of predictions of y^i given only the values of truly exogenous variables, or of some models $\bar{f}^i$: $X \to Y^i$ based on $f^i\colon X \to Y^i$. This may be done by defining $\bar{f}^i = \varphi^i \cdot f^i$ where $\varphi^i\colon X \to X$ is some naive extension of the model: that is φ^i maps the value of each exogenous variable to itself, and replaces each link variable by an estimate based on a naive model of one of the types specified above. This will also be considered.

6.2 NUMERICAL METHOD

It is clear that the models of the individual agents, f^i, are nonlinear, and thus not explicitly solvable by direct methods. The obtaining of actual solutions is thus necessarily a trial and error operation, and therefore perhaps worth some comment. This section outlines the general properties of the method used, from the viewpoint of understanding the computation procedure written for this study.

Iterative solution methods are best classified according to their power, where a powerful method is interpreted as one which reaches a solution after a small number of iterations; since the more powerful methods must do more at each iteration, they naturally tend to be more complex at each stage. Thus it does not follow that the more powerful methods are the more useful. Tests were made of various methods along the power spectrum, and it was found that one of the most powerful, suggested by Saaty and Bram, was typically the most successful in reaching a solution—despire its expected lower robustness. This was therefore used, in a modified form, for all solutions.

Basic Procedure

The basic procedure for solving a system of equations is best developed from the single equation case. Here the method essentially approximates the equation to be solved by its tangent at some trial solution point, obtaining the next trial solution from the intersection of this tangent with the axis. Thus if the equation is $f(x) = 0$ and $x(k)$ is a trial solution, $f(x)$ is replaced by its linear approximation about $x(k)$,

$$f(x) = f(x(k)) + f'(x(k))(x - x(k)),$$

and the next trial solution is given by

$$x(k + 1) = x(k) - f(x(k))/f'(x(k)) .$$

To keep matters simple it is assumed that f' exists and is nonzero everywhere; in fact almost everywhere is sufficient if one makes an obvious change in the algorithm. (The symbols f and x used here are purely abstract, and not those of our specific model.)

It is clear from the completeness of the real line that if the sequence $x(k) \rightarrow \bar{x}$ then $f(\bar{x}) = 0$, and $\bar{x}$ is a solution, so all one need check is that the sequence $x(k)$ converges, that is

$$|x(k + 1) - x(k)| \rightarrow 0 .$$

This is proved by a theorem of Saaty and Bram. The theorem shows this by placing sufficient conditions on the initial trial solution $x(0)$, say $x(0) \in S$, and showing that S is reasonably large, that is

$$\sup \left\{ x(0) - \bar{x} \mid x(0) \in S \right\} > 0 .$$

Unfortunately the restrictions on $x(0)$ are not much use in suggesting an appropriate initial value, but do give some information on the speed of convergence:

$$x(k) - \bar{x} \leqslant \beta (2\alpha)^{2k-1} / 2^{k-1} ,$$

where α and β are constants such that

$$0 < \alpha < \tfrac{1}{2}, \ \beta \geqslant |f(x(0))|/f'(x(0))| .$$

In the general case where $f: R^m \rightarrow R^m$ one proceeds analogously, and approximates the hypersurface representing each equation by its tangential hyperplane at some trial solution point, obtaining

$$f(x) = f(x(k)) + D(k)(x - x(k)) \ ,$$

where $D(k)$ is jacobian of f evaluated at $x(k)$, then takes

$$x(k + 1) = x(k) - D(k)^{-1} f(x(k)) \ .$$

The proof that this is a satisfactory procedure, that is that $x(k) \to \bar{x}$, is now a direct parallel to that of Saaty and Bram in the scalar case, provided the right metric is used. This turns out to be the maximum absolute value metric, that is

$$\|x(k + 1) - x(k)\| = \max \left\{ |x_i(k + 1) - x_i(k)| \, i = 1, \ldots m \right\}$$

Modifications

There are a number of possible modifications to this basic method. For example one may save work at each iteration by using the jacobian evaluated at the initial trial solution, $D(0)$, in each iteration k instead of $D(k)$. This however results in an unacceptable drop in robustness—that is convergence requires $x(0)$ nearer to $\bar{x}$. A more valuable modification, which is used, is the introduction of a damping factor $\gamma \in [0, 1]$ to give

$$x(k + 1) = x(k) - \gamma D^{-1}(k) f(x(k)) \ .$$

It is not difficult to show that this produces greater robustness, which is needed, at the cost of slower convergence. This second modification is used where necessary.

A further point worth noting is that unlike most methods the one discussed here uses information from all the equations for each modification of a trial solution, thus involving repeated matrix inversions. It is then more appropriate for small dimensional but highly interdependent models such as these, than for large but sparse models, such as the typical aggregate model.

Again, the model of the nonproducing agent is considered separately. This poses only a minor problem, for it involves virtually no simultaneity, and so may (almost) be solved directly, by recursion. The simultaneity that does arise is in the set of equations determining consumption and consumer prices, for consumption depends on relative prices and thus (nonlinearly) on aggregate price, while this in turn is the sum of individual prices weighted by individual consumptions. This simultaneity is of relatively minor importance since it arises only through the need to weight the various components of an aggregate. For this reason the problem is artificially avoided by using lagged instead of current values of consumption as weights in the computation of aggregate price, and making an approximate check by recalculating this from the current values of consumption thus generated. As the two figures are always very close, the maximum difference being about one-half of one percent, this seems an acceptable approximation.

6.3 PARTIAL SOLUTIONS

According to the ideas developed in the last two sections the individual sectoral models are now solved and assessed, bearing in mind that these relate to conditional predictions, conditional that is on the values of the link variables. This is done for the four periods (or quarters) following the sample set, identified by $t = 1, \ldots 4$.

Interpretation

There is of course a problem of determining the statistical significance of an assessment based on a small number of experiments, and one cannot hope to answer this in a formal sense here. All results derived from solutions of the model must be interpreted as interesting indications rather than rigorously specified statistical statements, and also as examples of the type of quantitative analysis which is possible in the general equilibrium framework proposed. All solutions then seek to provide concrete examples, or a tested methodology, rather than to answer specific questions. In this sense the purpose of the study is to provide a framework in which more substantive questions may be considered.

Producers

The results of these experiments for producers are given in Appendix C, and summarized in Table 6-1. For each period ($t = 1 \ldots 4$) and for each variable ($h = x$ (output) and z (profits)) this gives the measures of the errors of prediction of the main model, $E_h(t)$, together with the standards of comparison, or measure of the errors of prediction of the composite naive model, $E_h^0(t)$. The table also gives the comparable measures for the absolute accuracy of the models, that is for the extended models, $\bar{E}_h(t)$ (the extensions φ^i used are discussed below).

Table 6-1. Partial Solutions

t	$E_x(t)$	$E_x^0(t)$	$\bar{E}_x(t)$	$E_z(t)$	$E_z^0(t)$	$\bar{E}_z(t)$
1	0.020	0.039	0.045	0.152	0.173	0.133
2	0.021	0.038	0.025	0.197	0.365	0.176
3	0.033	0.080	0.040	0.146	0.159	0.226
4	0.099	0.053	0.064	0.225	0.197	0.233

The general conclusion from this must be that the individual agents' models are, given the information they use, good predictors of agents' behavior. This pattern is clear for all periods other than the last, which is more confusing. (The last period however is interesting in that it is a period of particularly violent change: for example aggregate unemployment rose by two-thirds.)

To be specific, the model's predictions of output are more accurate than those produced by any naive model for nearly all agents in the first three periods, and for half of the agents in the fourth. Overall, the output prediction of the real model is better than the best of the naive models in the first three periods, substantially so in the third, but somewhat worse in the fourth. In terms of profit predictions the picture is similar: the real model is better than the best of the three naive models for the first three periods, substantially so in the second, and slightly worse in the fourth.

Because of the nature of the composite naive model the real sectoral models have thus passed some reasonably stringent tests, and are therefore considered satisfactory for incorporation into the general equilibrium system.

As noted earlier, this conclusion does not imply that the sectoral models would make practically useful predictors, for it is possible that they are accurate only because they use illegitimate informaton, in the form of the link variables. Although it is not directly relevant here, this is also considered. As indicated, this is best done by specifying some naive extension function φ^i: $X \to X$ for the model f^i, then considering the modified model $\varphi^i \circ f^i \colon X \to Y^i$. For this to be valid one must make φ^i as simple as possible, which suggests that each link variable be replaced by its previous value, so $\varphi^i \circ f^i$ is defined on a genuinely exogenous set.

Such a procedure (in fact it is merely the first stage in the general equilibrium solution process discussed in the following chapter) generates the values $\bar{E}_h(t)$ in Table 6-1. From these it is apparent that this makes little difference to the accuracy of prediction: for both output and profits the modified measure $\bar{E}_h(t)$ is close to the original measure $E_h(t)$, and is actually lower in two of the four periods.

A final point concerns the alternative profits hypothesis. Chapter 4 considered using Evans' quasi-behavioral explanation of profits instead of the definitional formulation. The preceding experiments were therefore repeated using this formulation to give the following values of the measure equivalent to $E_z(t)$ in the four periods:

$$(0.555, 0.425, 0.323, 0.503) \ .$$

Comparing this vector with the values in Table 6-1 of $E_z(t)$ obtained from the profits identity it is clear that the quasi-behavioral formulation is far inferior: in each time period it produces measures substantially greater than (on average over twice the magnitude of) those produced by the identity formulation. In view of the conceptual problems of this alternative this is perhaps not surprising, but provides an interesting confirmation. Of course it gives the same figures for $E_x(t)$, since (in the current period) output is separable from profits (but not vice versa), as may be seen from the specification of the model.

Consumer
Finally, the model of the consumer, or nonproducing agent, f^0, deserves mention: the investigation so far has been only for the producing agents. This is not considered in detail, for this model has little simultaneity (and on this see the end of Section 6.2) as may be seen from Chapter 4; further, the individual equations fit the data in the sample period very closely, as may be seen from Chapter 5. Together these properties provide a very good indication of the accuracy of the model.

Chapter Seven

General Equilibrium

The preceding chapter considered the partial solution of the model, that is the solutions of the various agents' action rules, and showed that the specification of these rules is satisfactory in that their predictions agree with observable reality. This of course is only of indirect interest: what is of more direct interest are the stability and comparative static properties of the whole model.

The general equilibrium comparative static properties are given in an abstract setting simply by evaluating the function $F(x)$ for various values of the characteristics x. In a practical sense however this may be quite difficult: for example in this model it involves the solution of over 100 nonlinear simultaneous equations. One should not therefore attempt to solve these purely as mathematical relations, but instead make use of Walras' vital link between the mathematical and the economic solution of the system: this is the essence of Walras' tatonnement, 'a theory of the process by which the market mechanism solves the equilibrium equations' [p. 520].

Since the concept of a model developed in Chapter 2 embodies a natural specification of how the economy moves (or solves its equations), one need only follow this. That is to say one should generate the sequence of states

$$(y, f(y;x), f(f(y;x);x), \ldots)$$

where y is some given equilibrium and x is the characteristic one is interested in, and see whether this has a limit. If it has, then, assuming uniqueness, this must be $F(x)$; if it has no limit then the system is unstable, and comparative statics are irrelevant. Comparative statics are thus generated as a byproduct of the investigation of stability; it is for this very practical reason, as well as its logical priority, that stability is considered before comparative statics.

The chapter commences with a theoretical examination of the nature of the dynamics of the model, and then considers the measurement of stability and the stability properties; it concludes with a discussion of the accuracy and consistency of the general equilibrium solutions of the model.

7.1 DYNAMIC PROCESS

As was made clear in Chapter 2, the dynamic or stability process of the model is naturally defined: agents move if so doing benefits them unilaterally. In the abstract setting this was fully discussed in Chapter 2, where it was also noted that for more useful economic information one must make more concrete economic specifications. This has now been done (in Part II), so one is able to be more specific about the dynamics of the model. The conceptual differences between the Walrasian and natural dynamics have already been discussed, particularly the fundamental difference that the former uses an auctioneer while the latter is based on the actions of individual agents. Since the Walrasian process provides a most valuable point to start from, the mechanics of the natural process will be developed from this.

Walrasian
In the Walrasian model of production adjustment is entirely through prices, and the change of these depends on aggregate excess demands. Denote the price of commodity i, that is of the commodity produced by agent i, in some stage s of the process by $p_i(s)$. Since endowments are fixed, excess demands depend only on prices, so one may write the excess demand for commodity i at stage s of the process as

$$g_i(p(s)) \equiv g_i(p_0(s), \ldots p_m(s)) \ .$$

(The n agents are now labelled $0, \ldots m$, so the consumer is agent 0 and producers are agents $1, \ldots m$.) Equilibrium is defined as the state in which excess demands are all zero, and adjustment takes place to achieve this.

To be specific, the process is analogous to that for an exchange economy considered in Section 2.3. In a simple form this says that the change in prices from one stage in the process to the next is proportional to the excess demands, that is

$$\Delta p_i(s+1) \equiv p_i(s+1) - p_i(s) = a_i g_i(p(s)) \ , \quad i = 0, \ldots m \quad ,$$

where the a_i are positive numbers, or in an obvious vector notation,

$$\Delta p = Ag \ ,$$

where A is a diagonal matrix with (diagonal) elements $a_0, \ldots a_m$. (It is straightforward to extend this to the more general form which ensures that prices are nonnegative, and replaces the linear functions a_i by arbitrary increasing sign-preserving functions.)

Intermediary

Such a process not only depends on the existence of the auctioneer, but also requires him to be given, somehow, the adjustment coefficients $a_0, \ldots a_m$. As an intermediary step to the natural process it is constructive to consider a modification of this in which the a_i's do not have to be specified exogenously, but instead are implicit in the aggregate excess demand functions, and thus in the individual agents' behavior. This process chooses prices directly, so that excess demands would individually be zero if there were no interaction between the markets. That is, $p_i(s + 1)$ is chosen so that

$$g^i[p_0(s), \ldots p_{i-1}(s), p_i(s + 1), p_{i+1}(s), \ldots p_m(s)] = 0,$$

or more concisely,

$$g^i [p_i(s + 1), p_{(i)}(s)] = 0 \ ,$$

where, as before, $p_{(i)}$ is the m-vector $(p_0, \ldots p_{i-1}, p_{i+1}, \ldots p_m)$, which is of course taken as given.

Now prices are not explicitly adjusted in response to excess demands, though clearly they are implicitly adjusted in this way. One may equivalently write the adjustment process as

$$\Delta p_i(s + 1) = h^i [g^i, p_i(s), p_{(i)}(s)]$$

where h^i is some adjustment function implicitly defined by

$$g^i [p_i(s) + h^i[g^i, p_i(s), p_{(i)}(s)], p_{(i)}(s)] = 0 \ ;$$

indeed a further way to write this is as

$$p_i(s + 1) = \tilde{h}^i[p_i(s), p_{(i)}(s)] \equiv \tilde{h}^i[p(s)]$$

where $\tilde{h}$ is defined in an obvious way. (These restatements are purely formal—it is assumed that the excess demand function has the usual desired properties.)

The relevant difference is that current prices affect the change in price directly, as well as through their influence on current excess demand; this is of course illustrated more concretely in the example in Section 2.3. However, if one assumes the necessary continuity and monotonicity of the excess demand function, the two processes become equivalent in the neighborhood of the equilibrium. To see this, totally differentiate the excess demand function (at equilibrium) to obtain

$$dg^i = \frac{\partial g^i}{\partial p_i} dp_i + \sum_{j \neq i} \frac{\partial g^i}{\partial p_j} dp_j = 0$$

or

$$dp_i = -\left[\frac{\partial g^i}{\partial p_i}\right]^{-1} \sum_{j \neq i} \frac{\partial g^i}{\partial p_j} dp_j \; ;$$

one has therefore

$$\Delta dp_i = -\left[\frac{\partial g^i}{\partial p_i}\right]^{-1} \left[\frac{\partial g^i}{\partial p_i} dp_i + \sum_{j \neq i} \frac{\partial g^i}{\partial p_j} dp_j\right] = -\left[\frac{\partial g^i}{\partial p_i}\right]^{-1} dg^i \equiv a_i \, dg^i$$

or

$$\Delta p = Ag \; .$$

This is of exactly the same form as in the Walrasian process, the difference of course being that A is now determined naturally, while previously it had to be given exogenously.

Natural

Finally, the natural process is recalled from Chapter 2. This no longer relies solely on price, but now on all aspects of the agents choice, y^i, and environment, $y^{(i)}$, so one has the process

$$y^i(s+1) = f^i(y(s)) \equiv f^i(y^i(s), y^{(i)}(s)) \; ,$$

where f^i is agent i's observed action rule. Formally then, this is immediately equivalent to the intermediate process: one has simply replaced p with y, and g with f. At a more fundamental level there are many differences. The most important, which has already been discussed at some length, is that this process is entirely free from the auctioneer, and that it does not depend on any arbitrary definition of equilibrium; in other words, all adjustment is made by individual agents in an optimizing manner, and it is this process itself which determines equilibrium.

The more practical difference is that price is no longer the only aspect of the environment which agents may consider when taking actions.

Indeed, agents may take account of any aspects of any other agents' actions which they find useful: the aspects which fall into this set are those which are revealed in the agents' behavior, as represented in the specific model developed in Part II. These are then simply the horizontal and the vertical linkages in the model, and include such variables as outputs, prices, and so on.

In a sense then the natural model encompasses both the Walrasian process which achieves all adjustment through prices, and the Leontief process which achieves adjustment in a similar way through quantities (using the terms 'Walrasian' and 'Leontief' in their usual senses—though Walras also studied adjustment through quantities and price dynamics may be considered in the Leontief system). In so far as agents are observed to take account of this wider environment this process may reasonably be considered as more realistic. In that it uses more information at each stage it may also be presumed to be more efficient. For example, Koopmans has shown that the price system alone may not even solve the decision making problems of a single producer-consumer 'Robinson Crusoe' economy.

7.2 STABILITY PROPERTIES

With this more detailed understanding of the stability process one may proceed to attempt to measure its efficacy. Since this is to be a quantitative measurement, it must be by experiment. The experiment which is relevant is clear: one must prescribe some characteristics x and some initial state y, and compute the sequence

$$(y, f(y;x), f(f(y;x);x), \dots)$$

which would be followed by the economy. In other words, use the knowledge of disequilibrium action which is implied by observable equilibrium behavior to simulate the unobservable disequilibrium adjustment path of the economy. As is usual in an inductive approach, the experiment is performed various times (that is with different x or y) to obtain a richer knowledge.

Specification

The first question to consider then is the specification of the characteristics x and initial states y for the experiment. Since, as has been made clear, the results of the stability experiments are to be used in the comparative statical, or predictive, experiments, it is appropriate to consider characteristics x for which the economy's equilibrium is known. This restricts one to use the same four sets of data as were used for the partial solutions in Chapter 6, and so these are used for all experiments. Of course the general comments of Section 6.3 continue to apply—that is the experiments are designed to give a concrete example, or tested methodology, rather than to answer specific questions. Thus four values of x are considered, these being the values of the exogenous variables in the four quarters following the sample period.

One could specify the initial states $y(0)$ completely arbitrarily, but the main point of interest is whether the economy is stable with respect to states from which it is likely to commence; this is, loosely speaking, an intermediate stage between local and global stability. It is natural to assume that in the period (of real time) t the economy starts from the state at which it was in equilibrium in the preceding period, $t - 1$. This specification of the initial states is then made.

Now that real time as well as adjustment time is introduced the notation must be extended. Denote the state y in the *period* of real time t and *stage* of adjustment s by $y(t, s)$, and the characteristics and equilibrium state in the period t by $x(t)$ and $y(t)$ respectively. The experiment is then performed for the values $t = 1, \ldots 4$, and for each of these characteristics $x(t)$ and initial state $y(t, 0) = y(t - 1)$ are specified; one then studies the sequence

$$(y(t - 1), f(y(t - 1); x(t)), f(f(y(t - 1); x(t)); x(t)), \ldots) \ .$$

This is done by direct computation: one has the given vectors

$$y(t - 1) = (y^0(t - 1), \ldots y^m(t - 1)), x(t) = (x^0(t), \ldots x^m(t)) \ ,$$

so using the $f = (f^0, \ldots f^m)$ specified in Part II, one computes

$$y^i(t, 1) = f^i(y(t - 1), x^i(t))$$

and thus $y(t, 1)$, then repeats this for $y(t, 2)$ and so on.

Convergence

The only thing left is to decide whether or not this is stable, that is has a limit, and if so to form some impression of 'how stable' it is, or of its speed of convergence. Of course one cannot generally *prove* stability merely by examining a finite number of terms of the sequence, so one must necessarily use a certain amount of subjective judgment. (The only case where convergence would be assured is the happy one where the states in two successive stages were exactly equal—assuming that one knew this, or ignoring the fact that one can at the most only measure in rational numbers.)

The basic tool is the (second) Lyapounov theorem. Applied to this problem this states that if there exists some positive definite function defined on the states of the process and this is decreasing, then the process is stable. A positive definite function in this sense is some real-valued function $V[y(s)] \equiv V(s)$, continuous (in y) with continuous first differences (in y), which is nonnegative, and zero if and only if $y(s)$ is an equilibrium, that is

$$V(s) \geqslant 0, \; V(s) = 0 \Leftrightarrow y(s) = y \; ;$$

it is decreasing if

$$\Delta V(s) = V(s + 1) - V(s) < 0$$

(at least beyond some point, say s^*).

The standard formulation of this theorem is in terms of differential equations, but it is not difficult to see how it carries over to the difference equations of this process. Intuitively, if $y(s)$ is not the equilibrium then $V > 0$, but, as $\Delta V < 0$, $y(s)$ must be getting 'closer' to y; in other words V measures something akin to distance—it is of course a metric (for $y(s) - y$) apart from the triangle inequality. (The theorem is proved formally, and in some greater generality, by Allingham [1].)

One must now set about constructing an appropriate positive definite function V. Two points arise here. The first is that if knowledge of the equilibrium is to be used there are many appropriate functions, for example any metric, but if this knowledge is not to be used then one must be more circumspect. Since the stability process is being used to indicate the equilibrium, it is greatly to be preferred that no knowledge of the equilibrium is incorporated—and indeed essential if the process is not stable. The second point is that one wishes to attach some meaning to the actual values of V, which means that it should be free of units, and reasonably interpretable.

Since future states of the system are continuous functions of present states, and thus differences also, or alternatively by redefining variables, it is legitimate to introduce differences into V. The positive definite function is now specified as

$$V(s) = \frac{1}{\Lambda} \; [\underset{i}{\Sigma} \; \underset{j}{\Sigma} (\lambda_j^i \, \Delta y_j^i(s) / y_j^i(s - 1) \,)^2]^{1/2}$$

Here λ_j^i is the number of times that the j-th component of the i-th agent's action, y_j^i, is taken into account by any other agent in choosing his action, that is taken as a parameter. This is simply determined from the form of the model—for example the price set by an agent producing an (major) intermediate commodity is used once by all other producing agents, that is $m - 1$ times. Λ is simply the total of these (here about 80), or $\Lambda = \underset{i}{\Sigma} \; \underset{j}{\Sigma} \; \lambda_j^i$. Clearly V is only defined if all y_j^i are nonzero, and in fact this is ensured here by the implicit bounds of the model; if this were not the case then V could be modified in an obvious way.

It is immediate that V is continuous, as are its differences, and that it is nonnegative. If the system is in equilibrium, then no parameter, or any other variable, will change from one stage to the next, so $\Delta y_j^i(s) = 0$ for all i and j, which means that $V = 0$. Since the reverse implication also holds it is clear that $V = 0$ if and only if $y(s) = y$, so V fulfills all the requirements of a positive definite function.

It is clear from the form of V that this uses no knowledge of the equilibrium state y, so the first nontechnical requirement is satisfied. As for the second, it is also clear that V is unit-free, and indeed that its interpretation is remarkably simple: it is merely the root-mean-square proportional change in parameter values from one stage of the process to the next.

Armed with this positive definite function all one need consider is whether it is decreasing, that is whether $\Delta V(s) < 0$ for all s, at least beyond some point. It is clear that an equivalent procedure is to consider whether $V(s)$ becomes, beyond some point, sufficiently small for all s; the procedures are equivalent because both characterize $V(s) \rightarrow 0$, or $y(s) \rightarrow y$. The practical problem mentioned at the outset now arises: since one can only examine a finite number of stages, say $s = 1, \ldots S$, one cannot check that $\Delta V(s) < 0$, or $V(s)$ is sufficiently small, for all s beyond some point, but only for $s = 1, \ldots S$. It is then useful to make a more arbitrary definition of when the system converges, or becomes stable. For simplicity of interpretation this is expressed in terms of V, rather than ΔV: the system converges at the stage, s^*, where $V(s)$ first falls below some specified small positive number, ϵ, and remains below this number for all further stages which are examined, that is stages up to some specified S. If no such s^* exists then the system does not converge, or is unstable—strictly, (ϵ, S) -unstable. In other words, s^* is defined by

$$V(s) < \epsilon \ \ (\forall s | s^* \leqslant s \leqslant S) \ .$$

Results

One may now examine some specific results on stability. The adjustment of the economy for the four quarters following the sample period is considered, in each quarter starting from the equilibrium state prevailing in the previous quarter. We examine fifty stages of the process, that is set $S = 50$, and consider convergence to within two and half percent, that is set $\epsilon = 0.025$. The full results of these experiments are given in Appendix C; these are summarized in Table 7-1.

This table gives, for each period ($t = 1, \ldots 4$) the stage at which the process converges, $s^*(t)$, when of course V will be (slightly) below ϵ, and also the 'amount of divergence' which remains at the last stage considered, that is $V(t, S)$; finally, as an indication of the amount of adjustment required, the table gives the initial amount of divergence, $V(t, 1)$.

The most immediate and general result which emerges is that the system appears to be stable, and indeed highly so. Convergence is achieved after an average of only four stages, after which $V(s)$ continues to decrease slowly; after fifty stages have elapsed $V(s)$ is genuinely small—around four thousandths.

Table 7-1. Dynamic Properties

t	$s^*(t)$	$V(t, S)$	$V(t, 1)$
1	6	0.004	0.163
2	4	0.004	0.806
3	4	0.003	0.744
4	3	0.005	2.048

This strongly suggests that $V(s) \to 0$, or $y(s) \to y$. One cannot of course characterize this as global stability, for it has not been demonstrated from all possible initial states; on the other hand it is clearly more than local stability. It holds for the range of disturbance which is in fact encountered and which is quite large—large enough to generate initial values of $V(s)$ in excess of 2.000.

The relevance of these results is discussed together with that of the partial and general solutions in the following chapter.

7.3 GENERAL SOLUTIONS

Now that it is ascertained, with a reasonable degree of confidence, that the model is stable, one may validly consider its comparative statics. In other words, now that it is known that the equation $y = F(x)$ will typically have a solution for various values of x, one studies the properties of the solution.

There are many varieties of x which one might want to investigate for example the effect on unemployment in the food industry of an increase in consumer taxes on vehicles, and so on. In this study however we shall restrict our attention to the study of characteristics x for which we already know the economy's actual solution y, that is consider the predictions of the model as a whole. This provides a counterpart to the study in Chapter 6 of the predictions of the individual agent's models. Again it should be noted that we are mainly concerned with providing a tested method for the quantitative analysis of general equilibrium, rather than investigating more specific questions.

As has been indicated, the object is to examine the states $y = F(x)$ which the model indicates that the economy will actually move to when the characteristics x are those actually observed during the four quarters, and to compare these with the actual observed states in these periods. The manner in which this is to be done should now be clear: one proceeds exactly as in the study of stability, the predicted state simply being that state at which the system achieves equilibrium.

Accuracy

The main point of interest is the accuracy of the predictions. Again, the information available is too large to be reasonably interpretable, so one is faced with the problem of condensing this, to bring out its more important characteristics; naturally, the general observations of Section 6.1 on this point continue to apply. The concentration is again on output and on profits, but as one is now concerned with the economy as a whole one may validly consider more natural aggregates than were meaningful in Chapter 6: that is total product, x, and total profits, z. One measures then the proportional error of prediction of these two aggregates,

$$E_h = (F_h - h)/h \quad (h = x, z) \ ,$$

in each period (this happens to be well-defined). Note that one may now validly indicate the sign of the error, so this may be positive (for too high a prediction), or negative (for too low).

Again, a standard of comparison is needed. One may still use the naive models discussed in Chapter 6, but it is more instructive to compare the general equilibrium predictions with the more simple partial equilibrium predictions. For a genuine comparison each must use the same amount of information, so the partial equilibrium predictions must be those of the extended individual models—that is replacing the unknown link variables by their naive estimates, or lagged values, as in Chapter 6. From the nature of the dynamic process (or equivalently the computational procedure), it is clear that these are simply the corresponding measures given by the first stage of the process. Thus recalling that the convergent stage is denoted by s^*, the general equilibrium measures $E_h(s^*)$ are compared with the partial measures $E_h(1)$ ($h = x, z$).

Consistency

One conceptual problem remains—that of identifying total product. It was noted in Chapter 4 that this may be defined in two ways: total income, y^*, and total expenditure, y^0. Ideally, these should be the same, but in practice accounting inaccuracy may make them differ. We therefore have two distinct measures of total product. We do not explicitly use both, but simply consider the averages of these, that is

$$x = \tfrac{1}{2}(y^* + y^0) \ ;$$

in view of the presumed random nature of the difference this is a suitable condensation.

The question of consistency is however of some interest in its own right, for one should also consider whether the model retains the same degree of consistency (in this sense) as the actual (measured) economy. We therefore measure this predicted discrepancy $F_{y^*} - F_{y^0}$, separately. Since it is difficult to interpret in isolation this is expressed in terms of the actual inconsistency, giving, for each period, a measure of consistency

$$I = |(F_{y*} - F_{y0})/(y* - y^0)|$$

(it happens that this is always well-defined). Again this $I(s*)$ is compared with the corresponding measure for the partial equilibrium solutions, or equivalently that for the first stage of the process, $I(1)$.

Results

The results of these investigations in each of the four periods are summarized in Table 7-2. For each period t this gives the measure of the accuracy of the general equilibrium prediction of total product $E_x(t, s*)$ and the corresponding partial equilibrium prediction $E_x(t, 1)$, with similar measures for those of total profits, z. It also gives the measure of consistency of the general and partial equilibrium figures, that is $I(t, s*)$ and $I(t, 1)$ respectively. More detailed results are given in Appendix C.

The first implication of these results is that the general equilibrium predictions are, on the whole, surprisingly accurate. This is particularly apparent in the prediction of the key volatile variable, total profits, for here the general equilibrium approach definitely seems justified. In each of the periods investigated the general equilibrium prediction is significantly more accurate than the partial equilibrium prediction, typically so by a factor of three. This fact should be related to the earlier finding that the partial, or individual, models were themselves of acceptable accuracy, and definitely preferable to naive models. It is also relevant that, in a loose sense, disaggregation typically increases accuracy: thus the partial equilibrium models may be expected to be more accurate than a simple aggregate macro-model with the same type of structure. Taking these together, one may infer that the more complicated general equilibrium approach is, in practice as well as in theory, preferable (in the sense used here) to simple disaggregation (that is where there is no simultaneous interdependence between the submodels), and this in turn is preferable to a macro-approach.

What inaccuracy there is in profit prediction is not really determinate in sign in the aggregate, though it is instructive to consider the components of this: figures for the large nonmanufacturing agent are always too high, while figures for the manufacturing agents are predominantly too low (always so for the large engineering and vehicles agents).

Table 7-2. General Solutions

t	$E_x(t, s*)$	$E_x(t, 1)$	$E_z(t, s*)$	$E_z(t, 1)$	$I(t, s*)$	$I(t, 1)$
1	−0.006	0.055	−0.019	0.113	2.3	3.6
2	−0.072	−0.048	0.022	0.073	3.7	4.2
3	−0.015	0.015	0.094	0.166	0.5	1.7
4	−0.025	−0.009	0.002	0.009	0.4	0.2

The predictions of total product are also reasonably accurate, but only to about the same degree as the partial equilibrium predictions. This is to be expected, for the series is so stable that it is relatively easy to predict, so that the extra sophistication of a general equilibrium approach is not really needed. It is however of interest that predictions are slightly yet consistently too low.

Finally, the model appears to preserve consistency between total income and total expenditure, for the discrepancies between the two in the general equilibrium predictions are of the same order as those in the actual observed economy. However, it does appear that, as might be hoped, the general equilibrium solutions maintain a higher degree of consistency than the partial.

In summary, the added complication of a general equilibrium approach appears justified even in predicting the equilibrium values of broad aggregates; its value for investigating individual variables, and more particularly for investigating the process whereby these equilibrium positions are reached, is already clear. The further relevance of this is discussed with that of the stability analysis in the following chapter.

Chapter Eight

Conclusions

We have now fully developed and explored the tool (the model of Part II) for the quantitative analysis of general equilibrium. In this final Chapter we draw together the more important points which may have been learned from this analysis.

It has been stressed throughout Part III that its main purpose is to present a tested methodology for this type of research, rather than to answer more specific questions. Accordingly, the conclusions are necessarily of a rather general nature. In order to be more concrete, this chapter therefore takes up two examples of ways in which the analysis may be used. The first of these is more practical, and indicates the relevance of the study to the actual construction of decentralized planning procedures; the second is more theoretical, and shows how the analysis may be used to shed some light on the Marxian concepts of 'exploitation' and 'collusion.'

The chapter commences with some general implications, then considers these two examples, ending with some brief concluding remarks.

8.1 GENERAL IMPLICATIONS

The immediate implications of the partial and general equilibrium solutions of the model were mentioned in the two preceding chapters. These are now discussed a little further.

Partial Solutions

The general implication to be drawn from the partial solutions is that the individual agents' models are accurate: they provide good predictions of the agents' short run behavior, both in an artificial sense when they use illegitimate information and in a real sense when they use only legitimate information.

The relevance of this from a practical viewpoint is that this model may form a basis for more specific policy or forecasting models which seek to determine quarterly predictions of individual industry behavior. Typically, it is exactly this disaggregate quarterly information which is relevant from a policy or business point of view. Because of the nature of the aggregate constraints on government behavior, much fruitful government intervention (open or concealed) will differentiate between industries—easing the slowdown of contracting industries and steadying the growth of expanding ones. Similarly, the entrepreneur is more interested in which industry his resources may be most profitably employed, rather than some overall measure of profitability. There is no directly comparable work against which the accuracy of this model may be judged; however, this in itself, as well as the good performance of the model relative to naive models, suggests that this may at least provide a basis for more practical models. Of course modifications would be required, particularly to take account of the delay in obtaining recent values of some predetermined variables; these are not considered here.

The concentration on profits as the basic motivating force in the economy makes one further result worth mentioning. This is that the theoretically sound definition of profits, as a residual, is a practically more accurate predictor of quarterly profits than the less sound quasi-behavioral formulation—despite the former's practical drawback from being the difference between two similarly valued variables.

General Solutions

The overall implication to be drawn from the general solutions is that the model is stable: the natural tatonnement process solves the complex equilibrating equations between agents both efficiently and consistently.

While theoretical results on stability are quite well known, no other quantitative results are available at this time. It is important to note that there are aspects of stability which can be investigated quite naturally in this empirical framework, yet which are not apparent in the purely theoretical analysis. Firstly, the results apply to an actual imperfectly competitive economy rather than an abstract competitive one. Secondly, the actual path to equilibrium is shown, as is the number of iterations required; this is of particular relevance for practical applications. Thirdly, stability is shown from what may be interpreted as the real initial positions; it is therefore a stronger property than local stability and a more relevant one than (the even stronger) global stability. However, the main advantages of this approach may be not these quantitative aspects, but rather that it concerns a natural process inherent in the economy, rather than an artificial one added to the economy. Further, and implied by this, the process considered here uses whatever parameters are deemed appropriate by the individual agents, not just prices.

The relevance of this basic stability result depends on the acceptance of the two assumptions that the industry is the individual agent and that the time period of a quarter is a short one—effectively a Hicksian week. Like most assumptions in economics, these are not perfectly satisfied, though may be of sufficient validity to be useful. The ten industries (and one final agent) are taken to approximate the individual agents or firms (and consumer) for practical convenience, and a time period of a quarter is adopted for similar reasons, being the shortest period for which data is generally available; these matters were discussed in more detail in Chapter 3, and the assumptions must be considered as inevitable limitations to the applicability of the model.

Just as the partial result had potential policy implications so does this. However, this application, to decentralized planning, is more specific, and is taken up in the following section.

8.2 DECENTRALIZED PLANNING

The concept of decentralized planning proposed by Lange acts as a bridge between the organizations of capitalist and socialist economies. It is a way of simulating the action of a competitive economy to produce a desired efficient state, whatever the ownership of resources or existence of markets. It therefore suggests an answer to the fundamental question of how to combine equity with efficiency.

General Model

The general model of decentralized planning, as applied to this environment (in a slightly more abstract form), may be formalized as follows. There are a number of industries, each identified by the commodity it produces, and a consumer. Each producer has a production plan, that is a list of inputs (measured negatively) and outputs (measured positively) of his process; this must be technologically feasible in the sense of being in his production set (which is implicit in the models f^i). Similarly, the consumer has a consumption plan, or list of consumption commodities. A plan for the economy is a specification of all productions and a consumption. It is feasible if each production is individually feasible, and in addition the consumption of any commodity does not exceed its production. It is assumed that there is a preference ordering over consumptions: then a plan is optimal if it is feasible, and if it is maximal, with respect to this ordering, over the set of all feasible plans.

The object of planning is to produce an optimal plan. This would be straightforward if the planning agency were omniscient, but the basic premise of decentralized planning is that such is not the case. Specifically, it is assumed that the agency knows only the preference ordering (not the production sets), and that each producer knows only his own production set (not others', nor the preference ordering). This lack of knowledge is circumvented by a dialectical learning process which is the essence of the plan. The agency devises a draft plan which is issued to producers, who then, treating the information contained in this draft as a parameter, return proposals to the agency; on the basis of these proposals the agency redrafts the plan, and the process is repeated as many times as necessary.

The procedure may then be defined by the answers to the following four questions:

1. To which variables do the agency's drafts and producers' proposals refer?
2. How are the producers' proposals determined?
3. How is the agency's draft modified in the light of these?
4. When does the process end?

There are also a number of more practical problems concerned with the speed of communication, and whether producers will act as required, but these are not considered here.

Basic Procedure

A basic procedure is defined by the following answers to these four questions.

1. Drafts refer to prices of commodities, and proposals to production plans.
2. Each producer chooses a production plan that maximizes his profit, calculated at the draft prices, over his production set.
3. At each stage the agency changes the draft prices in the direction of the excess demand indicated at the previous stage (having somehow determined consumption demands at this stage).
4. The process ends when the iterations converge.

Of course for such a process to be well-defined one needs the usual restrictions: closedness and convexity of the production sets, and continuity and convexity of the preference ordering. Under these, and some more technical, assumptions, Arrow and Hurwicz show that the process will tend to produce an optimal plan—that is, after a sufficiently large number of stages, a price system will emerge that is optimal.

Modified Procedure

It is apparent that the basic procedure described above is a parallel to the basic Walrasian tatonnement process. The essential relevance of this study to the theory of decentralized planning is that a similar procedure may be defined which is analogous to the modified tatonnement process. As shown in Chapter 2, the advantages of this over the basic process are that it is a natural process with no need for arbitrary adjustment rules, and also that it uses all relevant parameters, not just prices. Just as these are helpful in analyzing the interaction of the economy, so may they be in simulating this; or in decentralized planning. In particular, the first means that the planning agency acts completely mechanically, and need not compute 'adjustment coefficients' or the like; the second generalizes Samuelson's [p. 232] observation that 'decentralized operators in a planned society should refrain from a literal aping of atomistic, passive, parametric price behavior. Instead of pretending that demand curves are infinitely elastic when they are not, the correct shape of the curve is to be taken into account.'

To conclude, it may be possible to define a procedure based on the modified process of this model. This study shows that such a process may be expected to be effective in the sense of achieving rapid convergence. The problem is to ensure optimality, that is essentially to choose parameters (components of the drafts) so that in the limit production is optimal. Of course if 'all prices' are the sole parameters one has this property (from the basic welfare theorem); on the other hand, if own prices are not a parameter it is easy to see that one need not. What has to be done is to determine the class of parameter sets which yield this property, then choose from this class the set which is most efficient in producing convergence. (Even if this class consisted only of 'all prices,' the modified process might still be preferable to the basic, for although it uses the same parameters it modifies these at each stage by the natural rather than the arbitrary adjustment process.) Thus it should be possible to simulate the existing equilibrium if the means of production were owned socially.

8.3 COLLUSION AND EXPLOITATION

The second particular aspect of the results which, for illustrative purposes, is explored further, concerns the apparent consistent downward bias of predictions of total product—as shown in Table 7-2 and commented on in Section 7.3. It should be emphasized at the outset that, with the information presently available, this is necessarily inconclusive; it should therefore be regarded as an example of the type of conclusion which might be available from this method of analysis rather than as a proven fact.

Theory

The overall model consists of interrelated models of the behavior of individual agents; as was seen in Chapter 6, these are, in a practical sense, accurate. The general equilibrium solution of the model is the state to which the dynamic tatonnement process converges, again in a practical sense. The tatonnement nature of this process means that this solution is the state at which the economy would come to rest if each agent considered the environment at each stage of the process as fixed, that is beyond his control. Since by its very nature the agent's environment cannot be directly controlled by him, but only by the other agents, this state is equivalent to the state at which the economy would come to rest if there were no collusion among agents, which may be called the 'natural' state.

If the general equilibrium solution consistently differs, in a practical sense, from the actual solution of the economy, this must either be because the models are not accurate, or because agents are not strictly following the tatonnement process—that is colluding. Since it is suggested that the first reason does not apply, one may infer that the second does, that is that there is in fact some collusion among the agents.

To investigate this further one must note a particular important facet of the effect of this collusion: it is to *raise* the level of output *above* its natural level (since the predicted, or general equilibrium, or natural level of total product is always below the actual, or collusion, level). In no sense is this observation at variance with the generally accepted position that monopoly necessarily restricts output, for this concerns monopoly *within* an industry. Because of the assumed homogeneity of the agents such a concept has no parallel in this model; what is relevant is monopoly (or collusion) *between* industries (or agents). This is a completely different problem, and there is no a priori presumption that it should increase or decrease output; one may however indicate why an increase is at least plausible.

As has been noted, there is a fundamental difference between the producing and consuming agents. The relevant aspect of this here is that while the underlying preferences of each may be represented by a utility function, that of the producing agents has, at least as a workable approximation, income (or profits) as its sole argument, while that of the consuming agent is defined on both income (or consumption) and on the amount of labor input.

Consider the producers first. It is generally accepted that their behavior is consistent with income maximization, and also that under the typical production and demand conditions (not too strongly decreasing returns to scale, or too steep a demand curve), income will be increased by an increase in output. It is assumed that this applies; it is indeed clear that most industries believe this to be the case in practice. Producers seek to maximize output, though they are of course constrained in this by the fact that they must buy inputs (labor) from the consumer—and sell the final output to him.

The nonproducing agent, according to the standard theory of the consumer, has a utility function defined on his consumption and his labor input, measured in some appropriate way, and this is increasing in the former and decreasing in the latter, at least in the relevant range. He maximizes this subject of course to a budget constraint relating his possible consumption to his labor input. If he is free to vary his labor by small amounts he will choose a position where the marginal utility of his consumption just balances the marginal disutility of his labor.

Now if there is no collusion, explicit or implicit, among producers the consumer would indeed be able to vary his labor input by small amounts (at least in a limiting sense), for different producers would be prepared to purchase different amounts—even if they would not all purchase any amount. If, on the other hand, producers collude, they will do so only to benefit themselves, which as has been seen, is to increase output. The simplest way to achieve this is to agree to purchase only zero or a 'large' amount of labor— which because of the consumer's presumed absolute aversion to zero consumption will result in the sale of the large amount. This then allows the producers both the inputs and the market required to increase output, which they accordingly do. This means that total product is increased beyond its natural level.

Observation
Such an hypothesis is consistent with the results: the tatonnement solution is one of lower total product than the actual, and also of lower profits for all industries other than the nonmanufacturing. Thus output is increased beyond its noncollusive equilibrium level, with the intended result that profits are also increased. The exception of nonmanufacturing to this rule is quite natural, for it is plausibly by far the most fragmented or competitive industry, and thus the one into which collusion can least readily extend. Further, its lower profit would be a natural result of the gain by manufacturing at the expense of nonmanufacturing when income is substituted for leisure.

It is apparent that this conjecture has much in common with Marx's analysis of the working of the capitalist system. Indeed one need only identify the producing agents with capitalists and the nonproducing agent with workers, and the general structure is equivalent. The particular findings however are very different: in Marx's analysis the collusion of capitalists forced the income of workers down, whereas in this it forces it up. The reason for this divergence is best seen by noting that collusion at the economy level may take two forms: it may alter the distribution of the total product, or it may alter the amount of the total product. Marx recognized only the first of these, which naturally yields the Marxian result. A priori however, both forms may exist, and it is clear that their effects on workers' incomes will be in different directions: the former to lower them and the latter to raise them. It is then a matter of fact which effect prevails. The analysis suggests a way of looking at this, yielding the result we have. In fact there seems to be no consistent difference in the distribution of the product in the tatonnement and actual solutions, both labor income and profits being higher in the actual economy.

In summary, it should be emphasized that this digression is intended more as an illustration of the type of analysis which may relate to the general approach than as a specific result. Subject to this, it would then suggest that collusion exists among producers to increase the total product, or that the capitalist system is inefficient in that it produces too much.

8.4 CONCLUDING REMARKS

Finally, it may be worthwhile to point out the main areas in which the analysis may be deficient, with suggestion for improvements, and to summarize the results.

Extensions

There are a number of specific points of this study where improvements may be possible. These have been mentioned in context; the present discussion emphasizes some of the more important.

At the conceptual level (in Part I) the most important extension would seem to be the movement from a tatonnement framework, where there is no trading out of equilibrium, to a nontatonnement one, which would allow such trading. This may be achieved by positing some institutional mapping, say g, which maps desired states into feasible states. Then given an environment, agents independently generate a desired state as before, but now (since this actually has to be achieved) this in turn is mapped into an achievable state (which is actually attained) by the 'institutions' of the economy. Instead of studying the mapping f then one must consider the composite mapping $g \circ f$. Since an equilibrium of f is achievable anyway (and since the restriction of g to achievable states must be the identity mapping), the question of equilibrium is trivial. The stability question however is more difficult, for a number of both conceptual and technical reasons; it is one of the more important open questions in economic theory.

On the model itself (Part II), there is always need for refinement of the underlying equations, for example through new theory, through more appropriate empirical representation of existing theory, through better estimation methods, or through better data. Besides refinement, or improvement of the existing structure, extension may be useful: this may involve an increase in the complexity (or number of equations) of the individual models, or the further disaggregation of the agents themselves. Perhaps the most valuable areas for refinement and extension are, respectively, the introduction of hours worked, and the disaggregation of the nonmanufacturing industry.

As regards the analysis of the model (Part III), there is clearly much more which can be done. It would be possible to extend all the solutions from four to many periods, and thus accept (or reject) the tentative conclusions with more confidence. It would be possible to perform actual comparative static experiments by simulating solutions for some fixed period with different values for exogenous policy variables. It would also be possible to investigate the real-time (as opposed to tatonnement-time) dynamics of the model by simulating many periods consecutively, possibly with the introduction of random shocks. Indeed, the main purpose of this study has been to provide a tested methodology, that is to bring the study to the stage where such extensions are possible.

Conclusions

This study has presented a quantitative analysis of economic inter-action, or general equilibrium econometrics. More specifically, it has proposed a fully specified model of an economy in which the formation of equilibrium is completely explained by the independent optimizing behavior of individual agents. This has mainly been concerned with presenting a tested methodology, and to this end it has been necessary to produce specific quantitative results; however, these should be considered primarily as indications of the type and order of conclusion which may be forthcoming from the approach, rather than as accurate results in their own right. With this proviso, the models of individual agents' behavior have been found to be accurate in prediction, the natural tatonnement adjustment process has been found to produce rapid convergence to a consistent equilibrium, thus being potentially useful for decentralized planning, and it has been possible to suggest the interesting result that the capitalist system is inefficient in that it produces too much.

Appendixes

Appendix A

Notation

This Appendix repeats, for reference, the symbols used in the concrete model of Part II. Further information may be found in the sections indicated in parentheses.

Industries (3.1)

(a	aggregate)		e	engineering
(m	manufacturing)		v	vehicles
n	nonmanufacturing		h	household
f	foods		t	textiles
c	chemicals		p	papers
s	steel		o	other

$$I = \left\{ n, f, c, s, e, v, h, t, p, o \right\}$$
$$M = I - \left\{ n \right\}$$
$$C = \left\{ f, v, t, o \right\}$$

Variables (3.2, 3.3)

b	consumer price		n	exports
c	consumption		p	price
D	consumption tax		Q	world trade
e	earnings		R	profits tax
F	government goods		s	stocks
g	intermediate demand		T	income tax
h	materials price		u	unemployment
i	investment		V	government transfers
J	government investment		W	government wages
k	capital		x	output
l	labor		$(y$	total product)
m	imports		z	profits

Where used, subscripts $(-\tau)$ denote date (number of periods before current) and superscripts (i, j) industry. Lower case letters denote endogenous variables and capital denote exogenous.

Parameters (3.4, 4.1)

α^i_{jk} k-th estimated parameter in equation j for industry i in producers' model

β^i_{jk} as for α, but in consumer's model

γ^i_j composite of estimated constant, seasonal terms, and residual in equation j for industry i in producers' model

δ^i_j as for γ, but in consumer's model

λ^{ij} input requirement of industry i per unit output of j

μ^i output base for industry i

ν^i weight for industry i

Appendix B

Parameters

This Appendix gives the numerical estimates of the parameters of the model as discussed in Chapter 5, together with the fixed coefficients discussed in Chapter 3. Estimates are presented in tabular form, giving, for each stochastic equation (((1) – (7) and (i) – (iv))) and each industry (**i**), coefficients (α^i_{jk} or β^i_{jk}) and their associated t-ratios for major explanatory variables, and coefficients alone for the three seasonal and the constant terms; also reported are the serial correlation (*SC*) and goodness of fit (*GF*) measures discussed in Chapter 5. The array, for equation j in industry **i**, takes the following form:

i	α^i_{j1} or β^i_{j1}	α^i_{j2} or β^i_{j2}	α^i_{j3} or β^i_{j3}	α^i_{j4} or $\beta^i_{j.4}$	first seasonal	third seasonal	*SC*
	t-ratio	t-ratio	t-ratio	t-ratio	second seasonal	constant term	*GF*

EQUATION (1)

n	6.81	0.000017	0.00117	-0.000206	-0.0183	0.0543	1.3
	23.2	0.4	3.3	2.9	0.0157	-0.0540	0.99
f	39.5	0.000156	0.000055		0.00240	-0.0351	1.5
	6.0	1.3	0.5		0.0197	0.266	0.99
c	28.1	0.000877	0.000203		0.0996	0.00110	0.8
	7.9	1.3	0.9		0.0315	-0.251	0.98
s	22.2	0.00619	-0.000732	0.000408	0.0366	-0.0531	2.1
	2.2	4.4	1.4	0.8	0.228	0.0245	0.95
e	26.3		0.000327	-0.000287	0.0325	-0.0455	2.0
	11.6		3.3	2.4	-0.00326	-0.0435	0.99
v	22.5	0.000399	0.000833	0.000558	0.0129	-0.0853	2.0
	2.0	0.6	3.4	1.4	-0.0223	0.0786	0.98
h	17.1	0.00113	0.000253		0.0316	-0.0536	1.0
	3.9	1.9	0.8		0.0110	0.468	0.96
t	41.1	0.000711	-0.000591		0.0278	0.0163	1.0
	16.0	3.1	6.8		-0.00184	-0.0709	0.99
p	11.3	0.00293	0.000114	0.000387	0.0316	0.0837	2.0
	1.3	3.0	1.3	1.5	-0.00549	0.120	0.98
o	21.5	0.00246	0.000339		-0.000980	-0.0132	1.2
	5.9	2.3	1.2		-0.00138	-0.0293	0.98

EQUATION (2)

n	0.000084	0.000051	-0.0941	-0.00998	2.0
	1.4	9.2	-0.0211	-1.69	0.98
f	0.000475	0.000386	-0.0490	-0.0556	1.5
	2.4	29.2	0.0149	-0.0759	0.98
c*					
s	0.00298	0.000116	0.0155	-0.0811	0.5
	5.4	4.3	0.0184	-1.04	0.79
e	0.000139	0.000432	-0.0230	-0.114	1.3
	1.2	8.0	-0.0400	-0.323	0.97
v	0.00112	0.000541	0.0521	-0.106	0.9
	2.5	9.6	0.0575	-0.775	0.85
h	0.000374	0.000191	0.0125	-0.0815	0.8
	1.0	2.8	0.00585	0.550	0.63
t	0.000320	0.00128	0.000699	-0.0849	0.8
	2.7	8.4	-0.0361	-2.70	0.84
p	0.000529	0.00101	0.00503	-0.119	0.9
	0.8	6.9	-0.00489	-0.467	0.94
o	0.00165	0.000353	-0.0341	-0.0401	0.6
	2.8	4.2	0.0150	-0.953	0.93

*Not applicable for industry c

EQUATION (3)

n	1050 2.7		0.124 0.7	138 -56.8	-13.8 -13.1	2.1 0.25
f	257 0.9	1060 3.1		49.1 - 2.65	36.4 -1072	2.7 0.57
c		293 1.4	0.0782 0.4	-14.8 1.19	- 1.18 -285	2.1 0.32
s	63.8 1.7		0.458 2.8	8.80 10.9	21.1 - 7.74	2.1 0.30
e	198 2.7	106 0.5	0.395 2.3	22.5 27.4	36.0 -125	2.4 0.46
v	12.4 0.4	168 0.7	0.424 2.2	-4.83 2.41	1.06 -162	2.4 0.28
h	51.9 0.8	305 1.3	0.355 1.9	-1.93 5.07	6.99 -302	2.4 0.32
t		809 2.2	0.0866 0.5	1.12 3.37	-28.4 -806	2.2 0.62
p		564 3.1	0.327 1.9	0.448 0.592	-0.607 -564	1.8 0.45
o		163 1.2	0.321 1.7	0.490 -1.41	-1.70 -161	2.1 0.24

EQUATION (4)

n	2400 1.1	0.498 7.6			-89.3 -17.9	- 9.08 688	0.4 0.84
f		0.0176 3.2	0.101 3.3		-26.1 -15.5	12.0 400	0.4 0.69
c*	48.4 1.0	0.0204 2.7	0.174 2.5	0.854 3.2	3.58 - 0.0755	5.24 -137	0.8 0.44
s	183 2.0	0.0362 4.8			16.6 5.70	-11.8 -437	0.7 0.53
e	200 0.8	0.331 15.2	0.314 3.9		64.5 32.5	11.5 -5740	1.8 0.98
v	86.4 0.9	0.0282 2.8			15.1 0.765	- 6.10 130	0.4 0.24
h		0.0326 4.1			4.93 - 4.83	-10.1 57.2	0.3 0.39
t	2330 4.8				58.9 9.61	-39.4 -502	1.1 0.48
p		0.0675 21.8	0.0895 5.1		9.00 5.17	4.40 -954	1.5 0.96
o	193 1.1	0.0643 9.6	0.0307 1.3		13.8 - 1.51	- 7.79 -722	1.0 0.92

*Fourth variable for industry c only is l/u.

EQUATION (5)

n	0.0800 1.5	0.0118 1.0	0.499 3.2	-28.1 -42.9	-29.4 -157	1.8 0.97
f	0.0797 2.7	-0.00405 0.4	0.318 1.9	- 1.26 0.0962	- 0.105 5.27	1.7 0.96
c	0.0947 3.4	-0.0113 2.5	0.742 7.2	-10.3 - 5.71	- 8.37 20.1	2.1 0.86
s	6.12 0.0825 0.5 2.9	-0.00807 2.7	0.834 9.1	8.59 12.1	16.0 - 4.45	2.9 0.86
e	10.0 0.0927 0.7 3.5	-0.00244 0.5	0.142 0.8	-10.8 - 9.44	- 8.31 14.7	2.1 0.96
v	0.0140 0.5	0.00901 1.2	0.560 4.0	- 5.33 - 0.375	- 1.74 - 4.12	2.4 0.69
h	0.0249 1.9	0.00169 0.7	0.597 4.3	- 4.94 - 3.00	- 2.49 3.79	2.1 0.85
t	12.2 0.0449 1.4 1.6	0.0116 0.4	0.676 4.6	- 4.03 - 0.489	- 2.53 -29.6	1.9 0.93
p	0.0359 2.7		0.644 5.0	- 4.18 - 3.05	- 4.15 5.10	2.2 0.79
o	4.78 0.105 0.7 5.6	0.0153 3.3		- 4.09 - 2.97	- 2.58 - 8.68	2.1 0.96

EQUATION (6)

n*

f	0.966 18.1			0.00676 0.00336	-0.00272 0.0293	0.6 0.91
c	0.239 3.7	0.000338 0.5		0.00449 0.00330	-0.00155 0.730	0.2 0.34
s	0.585 5.4	0.000422 1.1		-0.00303 -0.00241	-0.00344 0.373	0.8 0.87
e	1.44 32.6	0.000187 1.7	-0.000103 2.3	-0.0133 -0.00944	-0.0104 -0.0406	1.1 0.99
v	1.30 125.6			0.000824 0.00112	-0.000008 -0.299	0.9 0.99
h	1.35 11.7	0.00151 3.5	-0.000054 1.2	-0.00173 0.000903	-0.0183 -0.502	1.1 0.99
t	0.887 42.5		-0.000032 1.1	-0.00167 -0.00117	-0.000160 0.136	0.3 0.98
p	0.731 20.0			0.00159 -0.000335	-0.000509 0.267	0.2 0.93
o	1.23 17.7	0.00152 4.6	-0.000111 1.4	-0.0172 0.00148	-0.00576 -0.415	1.7 0.99

*Not applicable for industry n

EQUATION (7)

	A	B	C	D	E	F	G
n			0.158	0.496	0.0439	−0.0409	2.5
			1.6	1.0	−0.0648	0.350	0.54
f	0.241		0.0588		0.0429	−0.0376	2.5
	0.6		0.5		−0.0455	0.949	0.57
c*	5.96				−0.0249	−0.0545	3.0
	0.5				−0.00711	1.02	0.23
s	0.0344	0.182		0.246	0.0295	0.0214	2.8
	0.5	1.7		1.1	−0.00237	0.563	0.47
e			0.160	0.279	−0.00454	−0.115	2.7
			1.1	0.5	−0.0932	0.615	0.53
v					−0.0406	0.0170	2.8
					0.0838	1.00	0.33
h	0.0975		0.0410	0.188	0.00771	−0.0117	2.7
	0.4		2.1	0.7	−0.0178	0.775	0.42
t	0.222	0.102			0.0244	−0.00619	2.9
	1.5	1.1			−0.00721	0.898	0.57
p		1.06			0.0584	0.0333	2.8
		2.0			−0.00517	−0.0779	0.63
o		0.455		0.226	0.0524	0.00296	2.7
		1.8		0.6	−0.0360	0.319	0.44

*First variable for industry c only is $1/\Sigma u$

EQUATION (i)

	A	B	C	E	F	G
f	0.146		0.451	−242	−46.8	1.8
	5.1		3.9	−21.6	474	0.99
v		−227	0.452	72.2	16.0	1.7
		2.4	2.8	77.1	263	0.84
t	0.0715	−241		−177	−115	2.3
	3.5	0.6		−107	455	0.95
o	0.313	−875	0.552	−129	50.8	2.3
	4.7	1.9	5.3	− 5.12	526	0.99

EQUATION (ii)

	A	B	E	F	G
f	1.00	2.00	−0.0147	0.00496	0.9
	8.9	2.7	0.00535	−0.305	0.92
v	0.107	0.444	0.00339	0.00605	1.1
	2.0	3.9	0.0134	0.807	0.45
t	0.348	2.07	−0.00791	−0.00370	1.1
	5.7	11.9	−0.00499	0.558	0.98
o	1.58		−0.00307	−0.00929	0.3
	25.1		−0.0131	−0.574	0.96

EQUATION (iii)

n	0.0167	0.736		-16.9	-38.5	1.2
	2.1	6.1		-26.0	143	0.86
m	0.0437	0.560		- 0.772	-10.5	1.6
	3.3	4.0		9.78	-67	0.97

EQUATION (iv)

n	80.8	0.523		-26.0	-16.9	2.7
	4.2	4.4		-22.2	8.04	0.94
m	479			36.3	-11.3	1.6
	34.0			29.3	286	0.98

CONSTANTS ($\times 10^4$)

$$\lambda = \begin{bmatrix} 1432 & 2807 & 2455 & 1795 & 1079 & 975 & 1263 & 1203 & 1842 & 1914 \\ 173 & 1132 & 130 & 0 & 0 & 0 & 0 & 6 & 14 & 0 \\ 308 & 621 & 2513 & 429 & 231 & 193 & 140 & 198 & 402 & 629 \\ 173 & 40 & 148 & 3289 & 1448 & 1247 & 2278 & 6 & 69 & 75 \\ 203 & 171 & 195 & 204 & 1495 & 533 & 322 & 153 & 201 & 215 \\ 168 & 3 & 0 & 4 & 16 & 1863 & 11 & 3 & 0 & 22 \\ 144 & 232 & 231 & 157 & 567 & 904 & 1553 & 99 & 35 & 199 \\ 88 & 81 & 69 & 14 & 99 & 110 & 38 & 4231 & 118 & 672 \\ 333 & 343 & 170 & 11 & 96 & 28 & 48 & 54 & 2438 & 210 \\ 376 & 198 & 163 & 89 & 307 & 544 & 285 & 131 & 48 & 1129 \end{bmatrix}$$

$$\mu = \begin{bmatrix} 2407 & 209 & 177 & 183 & 487 & 224 & 167 & 234 & 146 & 192 \end{bmatrix}$$

$$\nu = \begin{bmatrix} 6065 & 452 & 357 & 357 & 878 & 415 & 336 & 483 & 289 & 368 \end{bmatrix}$$

Appendix C

Solutions

This Appendix gives the partial and general equilibrium solutions of the model as discussed in Chapters 6 and 7. The first part presents the partial solutions. This gives, for each industry ($i \in I$), for each variable (output and profits—$h = x, z$), and for each period ($t = 1, \ldots 4$), prediction errors for the real model ($e_h^i(t)$) and for the best (in root-mean-square terms over I for each t and h) of the three naive models ($e_h^{0i}(t)$). The second part gives the results on stability. This shows, for each period ($t = 1, \ldots 4$) the measure of divergence ($V(t, s)$) at each stage ($s = 1, \ldots 50$). The final part presents the general solutions. This gives, for each period ($t = 1, \ldots 4$) and each stage until equilibrium ($s = 1, \ldots s^*(t)$), the measures of consistency ($I(t, s)$) and also, for each variable (total product and total profits—$h = x, z$), the measures of accuracy ($E_h(t, s)$).

$$e_x^i(t) \text{ and } e_x^{0i}(t)$$

t		n	f	c	s	e	v	h	t	p	o
1	e^i	0.013	-0.010	0.008	-0.001	-0.038	-0.019	-0.026	-0.018	-0.027	-0.012
	e^0	0.076	0.042	-0.054	-0.006	-0.013	-0.056	-0.018	-0.008	-0.032	0.014
2	e^i	0.009	-0.018	0.006	-0.030	-0.037	-0.020	0.015	-0.021	-0.026	0.001
	e^0	-0.048	-0.055	0.019	0.031	0.047	0.022	0.058	0.041	0.013	0.000
3	e^i	-0.016	0.000	-0.003	-0.089	-0.025	-0.008	0.029	-0.009	0.033	0.010
	e^0	0.014	0.116	0.005	0.113	0.000	0.143	0.021	0.036	0.120	0.021
4	e^i	-0.001	0.009	-0.005	0.274	-0.044	0.042	0.077	0.020	0.099	0.054
	e^0	-0.021	-0.040	-0.042	-0.058	-0.123	-0.025	-0.010	-0.042	-0.050	-0.014

$$e_z^i(t) \text{ and } e_z^{0i}(t)$$

t		n	f	c	s	e	v	h	t	p	o
1	e^i	0.176	0.017	-0.060	-0.274	-0.018	0.293	-0.096	0.083	-0.136	0.020
	e^0	0.132	0.015	0.131	-0.140	0.038	0.292	-0.317	0.225	0.033	0.071
2	e^i	0.137	-0.002	0.205	-0.076	-0.020	0.220	0.449	0.072	0.249	0.061
	e^0	-0.013	-0.023	0.076	0.192	-0.025	0.000	1.100	0.000	0.271	0.045
3	e^i	0.228	-0.011	0.162	-0.006	0.073	0.155	-0.263	0.012	0.131	0.137
	e^0	0.026	-0.057	-0.032	0.368	0.013	-0.172	-0.231	0.164	-0.020	-0.015
4	e^i	0.152	0.094	-0.160	0.376	0.063	0.471	-0.234	-0.002	-0.158	0.054
	e^0	-0.103	0.037	-0.059	-0.174	-0.030	0.349	-0.304	-0.237	-0.346	-0.105

s	V(1,s)	V(2,s)	V(3,s)	V(4,s)
1	0.163	0.806	0.744	2.048
2	0.499	0.039	0.074	0.056
3	0.123	0.031	0.054	0.015
4	0.063	0.012	0.025	0.018
5	0.035	0.007	0.012	0.020
6	0.019	0.008	0.009	0.020
7	0.011	0.010	0.010	0.019
8	0.011	0.012	0.013	0.018
9	0.015	0.014	0.016	0.016
10	0.020	0.015	0.018	0.015
11	0.021	0.016	0.019	0.013
12	0.023	0.017	0.020	0.008
13	0.024	0.015	0.019	0.004
14	0.024	0.009	0.016	0.005
15	0.021	0.004	0.007	0.006
16	0.016	0.004	0.004	0.006
17	0.008	0.005	0.005	0.006
18	0.004	0.005	0.005	0.006
19	0.005	0.005	0.005	0.006
20	0.006	0.005	0.005	0.006
21	0.006	0.005	0.005	0.006
22	0.006	0.005	0.005	0.006
23	0.006	0.005	0.005	0.006
24	0.006	0.005	0.005	0.006
25	0.006	0.005	0.005	0.006
26	0.006	0.005	0.004	0.006
27	0.006	0.005	0.004	0.006
28	0.006	0.005	0.004	0.006
29	0.006	0.005	0.004	0.006
30	0.006	0.005	0.004	0.006
31	0.006	0.005	0.004	0.005
32	0.006	0.004	0.004	0.005
33	0.005	0.004	0.004	0.005
34	0.005	0.004	0.004	0.005
35	0.005	0.004	0.004	0.005
36	0.005	0.004	0.004	0.005
37	0.005	0.004	0.003	0.005
38	0.005	0.004	0.003	0.005
39	0.005	0.004	0.003	0.005
40	0.005	0.004	0.003	0.005
41	0.005	0.004	0.003	0.005
42	0.005	0.004	0.003	0.005
43	0.005	0.004	0.003	0.005
44	0.005	0.004	0.003	0.005
45	0.005	0.004	0.003	0.005
46	0.005	0.004	0.003	0.005
47	0.005	0.004	0.003	0.005
48	0.004	0.004	0.003	0.005
49	0.004	0.004	0.003	0.005
50	0.004	0.004	0.003	0.005

	s	$I(t,s)$	$E_x(t,s)$	$E_z(t,s)$
$t = 1$	1	3.6	0.055	0.113
	2	3.4	0.049	0.075
	3	3.1	0.036	0.048
	4	2.8	0.022	0.025
	5	2.6	0.008	0.002
	6	2.3	-0.006	-0.019
$t = 2$	1	4.2	-0.048	0.073
	2	1.6	-0.052	0.058
	3	-1.2	-0.062	0.040
	4	-3.7	-0.072	0.022
$t = 3$	1	1.7	0.015	0.166
	2	1.3	0.009	0.142
	3	0.9	-0.002	0.119
	4	0.5	-0.015	0.094
$t = 4$	1	0.2	-0.009	0.009
	2	-0.0	-0.012	0.013
	3	-0.4	-0.025	-0.002

References

Allingham, M. G. [1] 'Tatonnement Stability: An Econometric Approach.'
    Econometrica 40: 27–41 (1972). [2] 'Equilibrium and Stability';
    (forthcoming).
Allingham, M. G. and Morshima, M. 'Qualitative Economics and Comparative
    Statics,' chapter 1 in *Theory of Demand* (Morishima). Oxford:
    Clarendon Press (1973).
Arrow, K. J., Block, H. D., and Hurwicz, L. 'On the Stability of the Competitive
    Equilibrium, II.' *Econometrica* 27: 82–109 (1959).
Arrow, K. J. and Hurwicz, L. 'Decentralization and Computation in Resource
    Allocation,' chapter 2 in *Essays in Economics and Econometrics*
    (Pfouts). Chapel Hill: University of North Carolina Press (1960).
Aumann, R. J. 'Markets with a Continuum of Traders.' *Econometrica* 32: 39–50
    (1964).
Basmann, R. L. Letter to the Editor. *Econometrica* 30: 824–826 (1962).
Cambridge Department of Applied Economics (CDAE). [1] *Input-Output Rela-*
    tionships. Cambridge (England) (1963). [2] *Capital, Output and*
    Employment. Cambridge (England) (1964). [3] 'Capital Statistics.'
    [Unpublished: revision of CDAE [2]] (1966).
Central Statistical Office (CSO). [1] *Standard Industrial Classification.* London
    (1948). [2] *Standard Industrial Classification, Revised.* London
    (1958). [3] *The Index of Industrial Production.* London (1959).
Christ, C. F. [1] 'Aggregate Econometric Models—A Review Article.' *American*
    Economic Review 46: 385–408 (1964). [2] *Econometric Models*
    and Methods. New York: Wiley (1966).
Debreu, G. *Theory of Value.* New York: Wiley (1959).
Debreu, G. and Scarf, H. 'A Limit Theorem on the Core of an Economy.' *Inter-*
    national Economic Review 4: 235–246 (1963).
The Economist. London (Weekly). [Recently 'The Economist Industrial Profits
    and Assets' has been issued separately each quarter].
Edgeworth, F. Y. *Mathematical Psychics,* London: Kegan Paul (1881).
Eisner, R. 'Capital Expenditures, Profits, and the Acceleration Principle,'

chapter 5 in *Models of Income Determination* (National Bureau of Economic Research). Princeton: Princeton University Press (1964).

Evans, M. K. 'An Industry Study of Corporate Profits.' *Econometrica* 36: 343–364 (1968).

Fisher, F. M. [1] 'Dynamic Structure and Estimation in Economy-Wide Econometric Models,' chapter 15 in *The Brookings Quarterly Econometric Model of the United States* (Duesenberry, Fromm, Klein, and Kuh). Chicago: Rand McNally (1965). [2] 'On Price Adjustment without an Auctioneer.' *Review of Economic Studies* 39: 1–16 (1972).

Hicks, J. R. *Value and Capital*. Oxford: Clarendon Press (1946).

Kakutani, S. 'A Generalization of Brouwer's Fixed-Point Theorem.' *Duke Mathematical Journal* 8: 451–459 (1941).

Keynes, J. M. *The General Theory of Employment, Interest and Money*. London: McMillan (1936).

Klein, L. R. *A Textbook of Econometrics*. New York: Row Peterson (1953).

Klein, L. R. and Goldberger, A. S. *An Econometric Model of the United States*. Amsterdam: North-Holland (1955).

Koopmans, T. C. *Three Essays on the State of Economic Science*. New York: McGraw-Hill (1957).

Koyck, L. M. *Distributed Lags and Investment Analysis*. Amsterdam: North-Holland (1954).

Kuh, E. 'Income Distribution and Employment over the Business Cycle,' chapter 8 in *The Brookings Quarterly Econometric Model of the United States* (Duesenberry, Fromm, Klein, and Kuh). Chicago: Rand McNally (1965).

Lange, O. 'On the Economic Theory of Socialism.' *Review of Economic Studies* 4: 53–71, 123–142 (1937–37).

Leontief, W. W. *The Structure of the American Economy*. New York: Oxford University Press (1951).

Longley, J. W. 'An Appraisal of Least Squares Programs for the Electronic Computer from the Point of View of the User.' *Journal of the American Statistical Association* 62: 819–841 (1967).

Lyapounov, A. *Problème Général de la Stabilité du Mouvement*. Princeton: Princeton University Press (1947).

Marx, K. *Capital*. London: Allen Unwin (1946).

Ministry of Labour Gazette. London (Weekly). [Now *Employment and Productivity Gazette*].

Monthly Bulletin of Statistics. New York: United Nations.

Monthly Digest of Statistics. London: Her Majesty's Stationery Office.

Morishima, M. [1] *Dogakuteki Keizai Riron*. Kyoto: Kobundo (1951) [2] 'On the Three Hicksian Laws of Comparative Statics.' *Review of Economic Studies* 27: 195–201 (1960).

Nash, J. F. 'Equilibrium in N-Person Games.' *Proceedings of the National Academy of Sciences* 36: 48–49 (1950).

National Income and Expenditure. London (Annually): Her Majesty's Stationery Office.

Negishi, T. [1] 'Monopolistic Competition and General Equilibrium.' *Review of*

Economic Studies 28: 196–201 (1960). [2] 'On the Formation of Prices.' *International Economic Review* 2: 122–126 (1961). [3] 'The Stability of a Competitive Economy: A Survey Article.' *Econometrica* 30: 635–670 (1962).

von Neumann, J. 'A Model of General Economic Equilibrium.' *Review of Economic Studies* 13: 1–9 (1945).

von Neumann, J. and Morgenstern, O. *Theory of Games and Economic Behavior.* Princeton:Princeton University Press (1953).

Prais, S. J.'Company Profits and Dividends, 1948–1956. *London and Cambridge Economic Bulletin* 22: 6–7 (1957).

Quandt, R. E. 'Small Sample Properties of Certain Structural Equation Estimators.' [Unpublished: summarized by Christ [2]] (1962).

Saaty, T. L. and Bram, J. *Nonlinear Mathematics.* New York: McGraw-Hill (1964).

Samuelson, P. A. *Foundations of Economic Analysis.* Cambridge (Massachusetts): Harvard University Press (1947).

Scarf, H. 'On the Computation of Equilibrium Prices,' chapter 8 in *Ten Economic Studies in the Tradition of Irving Fisher* (Fellner). New York: Wiley (1967).

Statistical Yearbook. New York: United Nations.

Statistics on Incomes, Prices, Employment and Production. London (Quarterly): Her Majesty's Stationery Office.

Theil, H. *Economic Forecasts and Policy.* Amsterdam: North-Holland (1961).

Wald, A. 'On some Systems of Equations of Mathematical Economics.' *Econometrica* 19: 368–403 (1951).

Walras, L. *Elements of Pure Economics.* London: Allen Unwin (1954).

Wold, H. O. A. *Demand Analysis.* New York: Wiley (1953).

Index

About the Author

Michael Allingham received both his M.A. and Ph.D. from the University of Edinburgh where he also was a member of the Department of Economics, then he was a member of the faculty of the University of Essex. In the United States he taught first at Northwestern University and then joined the faculty of the Wharton School, University of Pennsylvania in 1972. Since writing his dissertation in econometrics his main interest has been mathematical economic theory, particularly general equilibrium theory. He has published a number of articles in this field, as well as in the more general areas of mathematical sociology, politics, and public policy.